Cover: American Indian warriors of the C...

Photo Courtesy of the Azusa Publishing C...

1

Dedicated to Doris Anne,

DRUM
&
HOOFBEATS

Robert D. Bolen

Robert D Bolen

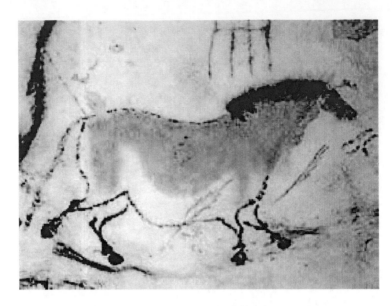

Ancient Cave Painting of the Appaloosa
Photo Courtesy of Wikipedia.org

Prehistoric Cave Painting of an Indian on a Horse
Public Domain

Zebra in South Africa
Photo Courtesy of Wikipedia.org

Wild Mongolian horse
Photo Courtesy of Wikipedia.org

CONTENTS

LIST OF ILLUSTRATIONS

The Spanish Mesteño (Mustang)
Public Domain

ACKNOWLEDGEMENTS

First of all, I want to thank my wife, Doris Anne for editing this book. She is excellent in English and grammar. Errors seem to vanish, when she looks them over!

I would like to express my deepest thanks to Teresa, owner of Azusa Publishing, LLC, in Denver, Colorado for all of the wonderful iconic Indian post cards that she has graciously allowed me to use in this text. The Curtis photos are superb. Pictures really make the book in my estimation. Her website ad containing gorgeous authentic Indian postcards is on page 178. I highly recommend her site.

I would also like to thank the Idaho State Historical Society for excellent pictures of Native Americans of long ago.

Thank you to Bonnie Fitzpatrick, my Graphic Designer for the wonderful job of creating the cover for this work. She does an excellent job. See her ad on page 179.

I have an additional source for photos and thank you so much, Wikipedia, who gave permission for the use of their photos and have allowed me the use of their gallery.

Last, but not least, my sincerest thanks to Ingram Publishing Company for their professional job of printing this fine publication.

the Author

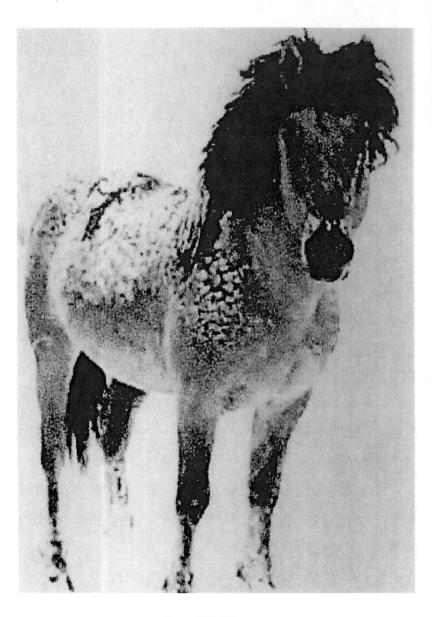

Spanish Mustang
Photo courtesy www.aaanativearts.com

FOREWORD

Horses were indigenous to America during the Pleistocene Period. Paleontologists theorize from the skull size that the first horses were zebras. The "Hagerman Horse" in Idaho is such an example. The last of the prehistoric horses died out in America sometime between 13,000 and 15,000 years ago at the end of the Pleistocene period, but the equus horse had already spread into Asia. Horses have pulled chariots, plows, and sledges. The modern horse was bred from wild varieties by Eurasians. One theory is that wild horses were hunted by the Indians and eaten and not ridden, and became extinct in America for thousands of years, but did thrive in Asia and Europe. Horses died out in the Paleo-Indian Period according to Archeologists.

Modern asses, horses, and zebras all belong to the genus, equus. They are the only surviving members of the family of equus that appears to have originated in North America that presumably crossed the Bering Straits to Eurasia thousands of years ago. One living example of the original genus equus is the Tarpan horse native to the Gobi Desert in Mongolia. DNA showed two strains of different species of the early horse brought to America. Most horses of the genus equus became extinct 10,000-12,000 years ago due to human hunters or climate change. I am of the old school that God created the horse and that it did not evolve. The Arabian horse was developed in the Middle East.

In the 15th century, The Queen of Spain commissioned Christopher Columbus to seek a new trade route to the East. He meant to bring Afro-Turkic Spanish–Arabian horses to the New World, but Sorraia horses were loaded on board, instead. Spanish conquistadors were responsible for bringing modern horses to the New World. Columbus brought horses to the Americas and found them useful in 1495 to attack a warring tribe. He recommended horses be on board sailing vessels bound for America from Spain.

Cortez in the 16th century was responsible for the first horses on American soil. Since then, the horse adapted very quickly into the American culture.

11

Wild Spanish Mustang
Photo Courtesy of Wikipedia.org

CHAPTER ONE
SPANISH HORSES
IN THE NEW WORLD

In 711 A.D., Berber General Tariq-ibn-Ziyad led a Muslim Army across the Strait of Gibraltar from Northern Africa and invaded Spain. The fierce Arab raiders rode in on Berber horses to attack the citizenry at night storming the Goth rulers of Spain and conquered them in a number of minutes.

The Arabs ruled Spain for eight centuries. The Moor reign was for the better in that they were advanced in Astronomy, Chemistry, Geography, Mathematics, and Philosophy. They modernized the cities. The Arab cities' architecture was ahead of the times. Cordoba was the most modern city in Europe when they ruled. The city had 900 public baths. Streets were illuminated. The Arabs built beautiful castles. Education during that time was universal, while Europe was illiterate. The Moors introduced paper to the world and three stringed instruments. They bred Iberian horses with Barbs from the Barbary Coast and a brand new breed emerged. Muslim rule culminated in 1492 A.D. with the eventual exit of the Muslims from the Spanish scene.

The Moors ruled and occupied Lisbon until the twelfth century, when they were defeated and driven out of Spain by King Alfonso Henrique's Army at the Battle of the Castle of St. George. Muslims fled the country leaving hundreds of horses behind.

When Christopher Columbus discovered America, he reintroduced the horse to the continent by bringing the first horses to the New World from Spain and starting a breeding colony in the Americas. He had planned to bring Andalusia horses, but someone switched to Sorraia horses, a more rugged horse to withstand the trip. They were later cross-bred with Mustangs. Columbus favored ranching over the quest for gold. He brought 6 mares, 4 jackasses,

Painting of Columbus Landing in America
Photo Courtesy of Wikipedia.org

2 she-asses, 4 bull calves, 2 heifers, 100 sheep and goats, 80 boars, and 20 sows aboard ship. The offspring of a male donkey and a female horse is a mule. A jackass is a male donkey and a she-ass is a female donkey. A burro is a small donkey used as a pack animal.

On his second trip, Columbus brought horses given him by Queen Isabella to the West Indies and introduced horses to the Western Hemisphere. If an animal died at sea, it was thrown overboard

In the 1500s, the demand for horses drove the prices up. In 1505, the King of Spain forbade shipments to the colonies because of the shortage.

Ponce de Leon sailed with Christopher Columbus on his 2nd voyage commissioned by Charles I, King of Spain to colonize Florida. Arriving near Charlotte Bay in 1513, he anchored his ships. Mounted on 50 horses, Ponce de Leon and his expedition embarked on to Key West and continued along the western coast. Ponce de Leon and his party of 200 settlers were ambushed by hostile Colusa Indians. During the melee, Ponce de Leon was struck by an Indian's arrow. In the fracas, some cattle and horses were lost. The party retreated to Cuba, where Ponce de Leon died and never ever found his "Fountain of Youth."

Velazquez ordered Cortez to Yucatan for conquest of land, riches, and slaves and was appointed as City Magistrate of Santiago. Cortez had sailed from Cuba with a flotilla of 10 galleons, 600 soldier, 18 horsemen, ten stallions and six mares on board. Bernal del Castillo, infantryman under Cortez, described: a Pinto stallion, black stallion, 14 Arabians, and two Andalusia, being transported in slings to keep them from breaking their legs. He landed on the shore of the Gulf of Mexico near Vera Cruz, Mexico in 1519, with the first modern horses in the New World. Horses weighed 700-800 pounds and averaged 14 hand spans high.

Spanish Galleons
Photo Courtesy of Wikipedia.org

Most of the horses shipped to the New World arrived safely. In the colonies some perished due to harsh winters. Some were eaten to avoid starvation. Some were killed by predators.

In 1519, Diaz served under Cortez aboard ship. He told the fable of a foal owned by Juan Sedęño, a wealthy Havana settler. The colt, whose name was El La Drone, had apparently strayed and was lost during the march of Cortez to Mexico City. The pony was seen for years running with a herd of deer. The pony stole a mare from a bunch of Spanish horses in order to start its own herd. Diaz's account has become legend. The fable said that El La Drone was the first Mesteño, (Spanish for Mustang). In Mexico, Diaz observed natives that hadn't seen a horse up to this time and believed the horse and rider to be all one animal.

Mexican natives under the rule of Chief Moctezuma of the Aztec Empire, believed Cortez to be an ancient god returned, the story from Aztec lore of the mythological feathered serpent, Quetzalcoatl, who sailed away centuries earlier and had promised to return from the East that very year and reclaim the nation. Cortez planned an assault against Moctezuma, whose enemy allies agreed to join forces with him. Cortez led 2,000 Tlexcaltecan warriors and 400 Spanish soldiers with horses, swords and muskets, which marched against the city and conquered the 20,000 natives of Cholula. Cortez's assault killed 15,000-30,000 Cholula natives.

When Cortez invaded Mexico, Indians killed one of their horses and cut it into bits to prove it was not a god, but mortal. The Aztecs soon discovered that horse and riders were not one being. Indians showed the horse to villagers to prove it was not a deity and presented the horseshoes to their idol. Indians had to conquer their fear of horses. Some feared horses or simply adored them. Indians worshipped horses and thought them to be sacred.

Painting of Hernan Cortez
Photo Courtesy of Wikipedia.org

Cortez's army arrived in Tenochtitlan November 8, 1519, at the Aztec capital of 200,000 occupants and its immense wealth. Moctezuma welcomed Cortez knowing that he could crush the Aztec invaders. Cortez was armed with horses, body armor, swords, muskets, and vicious war dogs. Cortez told Moctezuma that he and his men suffered from a disease of the heart that could only be cured by gold. Governor Velazquez sent a war party to arrest Cortez. In the meantime Cortez took his best men and left Aztec territory leaving Pedro de Alvarado y Contreres in charge. Spanish disease left bloody destruction over the next two years. The lust for gold burned in Cortez' bosom and caused the demise of the Aztec Nation. He defeated the governor's punitive forces enlisting them to fight under promises of rewards of gold. He bolstered his campaign with fresh horses and supplies.

Arriving at the capital, Cortez learned Velazquez had ordered the murder of the Aztec nobility, sparking a revolution. Aztec warriors attacked the capital, where Cortez had made his headquarters. He insisted Moctezuma address his people from a balcony, where the Aztec ruler was stoned to death. Aztec Indians rose up in order to save their city. Cortez and his army tried to silently escape, but they were found out; fierce fighting resumed crushing Cortez's forces. He lost 400 Spanish soldiers and 2,000 native allies on July 1, 1520 and 400 more soldiers also perished.

Cortez lusted for gold and had great wealth. In 1521, he again attacked Tenochtitlan, where warriors were positioned on the roof tops. He set the city on fire while the Aztecs were besieged with the smallpox. Cuauhtemoc, Moctezuma's nephew, had come to power after Moctezuma surrendered to Cortez August 13, 1521. Cortez, overcome by so much death of men and horses stated this: "God knows how much we miss them and how much grief their death causes us, because after God, horses are our only security."

Magnificent Spanish Mustang
Photo Courtesy of Wikipedia.org

In 1524, Cortez sent a message to Emperor Charles V. "I am dispatching ships to Cuba for supplies, especially horses." From then on horses were shipped to the New World nonstop for 50 years after Cortez's voyage. Spaniards brought Andalusia, Appaloosa, Arabian, Barbary, Iberian, and Spanish Mustang horses from Spain on board sailing ships to the American shores. The spotted Appaloosa horse is depicted on an ancient cave painting dated 15,000 B.C. in France. Appaloosas are believed to be a cross between the Andalusia and Barb horse. These fabulous horses were bred in Spain and brought to the New World.

When Cortez needed the Indians' respect, he had a stallion brought in to the arena, where a mare was tethered. Cortez had his men remove the mare. The stud snorted, whinnied, and pawed the air. The natives were terrified. Cortez told them that the stallion had been instructed not to harm them, since they came in peace.

Spanish armies on horseback conquered the Indians and Cortez attributed the victories to their god and the horse. They ran two horses through a village, and routed all of the villagers. Cortez thought the loss of one horse was equivalent to twenty men. After two years in Central America, a frail Cortez returned to Tenochtitlan and began to build Mexico City.

In 1525, Cortez marched into Central America in the rugged mountains intent on revenge for the death of a comrade. During the march Cortez's favorite horse, El Morzillo, a magnificent stallion, also called "The Black One" got a splinter in his leg. He reached the Island of Peten, left his lame horse with a Mayan chief and departed. Natives adorned the horse with flower garlands worshipping it, but it died of the wound. 100 years later, Spaniards returned to the island and found Indians still worshipping an image of a horse, their god of thunder and lightning.

Spanish Jennet Horse
Photo Courtesy of Wikipedia.org

Fernando De Soto imported one hundred horses from Spain for his 1538 expedition. One theory about horses left there is that in 1543 De Soto's horses were abandoned on the Mississippi, bred on the plains and were lost to civilization. Another theory is that they migrated westward to New Mexico and mated with horses of Cortez. Another theory was that six ponies escaped and migrated to the warmer plains of eastern Texas and that the mares gave birth to foals in the spring and four fuzzy colts were born.

They are just sagas. De Soto's expedition had 250 men with 1,000 extra mounts. Any number could have escaped, but no one can attest to that. Natural predators or the elements could have killed them. One saga of De Soto's horses was that the Indians pulled his horses' saddles and bridles off and set them free, then hunted them down with bows and arrows.

In 1541 A.D., Spanish Viceroy Mendoza employed Aztec Indian warriors for his army equipped with horses during the Mixton War in Mexico. The Indians rubbed their bodies with horse sweat in order to get the horse magic. This was the first time that horses were given to Native Americans.

In 1539, Coronado sailed with 237 horses. Coronado traveled to Arizona in 1547. Horses were introduced in Mexico, Central and South America. Wild horses still roam there today. When natives first saw horses it was a funny scenario. They tried to ride the horses and fell off. At first Natives feared horses and thought them to be gods.

In 1609, the first horses arrived in Jamestown, Virginia Colony in America. In 17th century England, France, Netherlands, and Sweden delivered horses to America. In 1629, 25 mares arrived in Massachusetts. In July 1, 1630, cattle and horses were aboard the Mayflower when she landed in the Charleston Harbor. Horses were brought to the east coast, in Florida and the Carolinas.

Palomino Horse
Photo Courtesy of Wikipedia.org

Wild horses roamed the east coast beaches from Delaware to Georgia, known as "beach ponies." Wild horses emerged in South Carolina on the seaboard, which may have escaped from Virginia. True living legacies of Spanish and American history, the small ponies that were wild horses of the **southeastern coastline** have a special mystique that intrigues and enchants thousands of visitors each year. They live among the dunes, maritime forests and salt marshes of a few places in Delaware, Georgia, Maryland, North Carolina and Virginia. These ponies have survived for centuries of generations against all odds in America.

Two herds of wild horses that make their home on Assateague Island at the Maryland-Virginia line are survivors of a Spanish galleon which wrecked off the coast of Assateague. These small, sturdy, shaggy horses have adapted to their environment by eating beach and marsh grasses and drinking fresh water from local ponds. These little horses are also "Beach ponies" and are wild. The Maryland herd is managed by the National Park Service and the Virginia herd is cared for by the Chincoteague Volunteer Fire Company, who purchases a grazing permit from the National Fish & Wildlife Service. The permit allows the Fire Company to maintain a herd of approximately 150 adult ponies on Assateague Island. The Fire Company controls the size of the herd by having a pony auction on the last Thursday in July. Each year, thousands of spectators come to watch the Saltwater Cowboys swim the pony herd from the Assateague Island to Chincoteague Island.

The wild horses of North Carolina's Outer Banks once roamed freely along the entire length of this coastal barrier island chain. They were isolated from human contact for nearly 400 years. Ponies descended from Spanish mustangs brought by the Spanish conquistadors to the Carolina coast. They have tenaciously survived this harsh and unforgiving environment over the years.

Medicine Hat Horse
Author Photo

CHAPTER TWO
PUEBLO REVOLT

The Spanish conquistadors expanded their territory into Arizona and New Mexico around 1540 and seized more than one hundred Indian villages (pueblos).

Juan de Onate had observed Plains Apaches along the Canadian River and forced the Indians to work their own land as serfs. Onate brought 7,000 head of cattle from Mexico. New Mexico was colonized by the Spanish in 1598. Onate founded the town of Santa Fe and pressed north in search of gold along the Rio Grande River. His sole purpose in colonizing New Mexico was to search for Cibola's gold, yet the missionaries, who accompanied him were determined to Christianize the Indians. Onate discovered the Pueblo Indians villages and settled among the farmers, but Onate's armies and priests conquered and enslaved them.

The Spaniards were cruel taskmasters of the Pueblo Indians who were forced to work as common serfs in the Pueblos. The ruthless Spaniards did not allow the Indians to ride or own horses. Spanish vaqueros (cowboys) worked the cattle. This kept the Indians from escaping on horseback and limited their movement. The Spanish hoarded the horses, but lost stock to coyotes, cougars, eagles and hostile Indians. If they fled, the Pueblos were surrounded by hostiles and had no place to run.

The following quote came from Comanche legend echoing the plight of the Pueblo People during their Spanish enslavement.

"Our responsibility was to be stable hands. We were literally slaves to the Spaniards and were the ones that fed the horses and cared for them. When the horse became an ally to the Comanche, it wasn't just a beast of burden. The horse really became a companion and a friend."

Taos Pueblo
Wikipidea.org

The first Spanish colony in New Mexico, San Juan de los Cabelleros, was established at the San Juan Pueblo, now named Ohkay Owingeh. It was a Franciscan enclave dedicated to converting the Pueblo Indians to Christianity. Juan de Onate crossed the Rio Grande and claimed the land north of the Colorado demanding grain from the Indians' winter storehouses. Onate established a colony for Spain called San Juan Pueblo de los Caballeros, after his patron saint, John the Baptist. Onate however was not a saint. The Pueblo Indians from the Tewa Pueblo shared their homes and food with them.

Onate forced the natives from their homes and established a colony across the river and made it the provincial capital becoming governor of the province of Pueblo San Gabriel de Yunque. During a winter storm, 30 horses broke loose and ran free.

The first to rebel were the Acoma Pueblo Indians. In December of 1598, a party of Spanish soldiers arrived at the Acoma Pueblo seeking food. The Indians welcomed and fed them. Things went well until the soldiers became aggressive. They rose up and killed 13 soldiers in the fighting. Their commander was Juan de Zaldivar, nephew of Juan de Onate, who would make an example of the Acoma Puebloans.

For revenge, Onate sent in 70 of his best soldiers to attack them. The Spanish Armies had the advantage with horses. In addition, they had steel helmets, body armor, pistols, swords, muskets and cannons.

The poor Indians had only bows and arrows. The Acoma Indians sent a hail of rocks and arrows down on the soldiers. Rocks were either thrown or hurled using bolos or slings. For three days they fought. The soldiers rolled a canon up the rear of the mesa and began firing into the village. Using canons, the battle became a bloody massacre and 800 Puebloans were slaughtered.

Juan de Onate
Photo Courtesy of Wikipedia.org

In 1600, Onate became overseer of ranches in New Mexico, while Jesuit priests colonized California with missions. They cut windows and doors in the pueblo to make it pass European standards. Spanish soldiers began to raid the neighboring pueblos taking anything of value. Wild horses ran rampant in New Mexico circa 1600 A.D. Domestic horses broke loose and joined the nearby wild bunch. Onate lost 300 ponies that escaped to join the wild herd.

The Pueblo Indians lived under oppression for decades under the Spanish. The Spanish forced the Pueblo Indians to work at hard labor and required that that pay taxes. Worst of all, the Indians' religion was suppressed. Franciscans proselytized the Pueblo Indians.

Slaves were compelled to build corrals and stables. Beleaguered slaves were forced to herd sheep and goats, while boys had to feed and water horses and clean stables. The Pueblo Indians became restless of tending the animals day and night. Onate ruled for twelve years, until 1610, when he was tried for cruelty to the Indians and banned from New Mexico, which was later overturned. Exonerated of all charges, he retired in Spain.

Rebellion of the Acoma Indians was long remembered; Tension continued between the Spanish and the Puebloans. The Spanish demanded food and labor of the Indians. The Indians objected to Catholic baptisms and many missions being founded.

Most Puebloans lived in peace alongside the Spanish due to the protection the Spanish provided against the Apache and Navajo Indian raiding parties, but some Pueblo Indians rebelled against the stronger Spaniards. These uprisings were quickly suppressed.

In 1623, Franciscan friar, Alonso de Benavides described seeing a Gila Apache chief riding a horse. Apaches owned a horse early due to theft or by capturing strays.

The Acoma Pueblo
Photo Courtesy of Wikipedia.org

In 1629, the Zuni Indians revolted against Spanish rule. The Spaniards treated the Pueblo Indians cruelly, forcibly proselytized them to accept the Roman Catholic religion. Spaniards in the southwest forced the Acoma, Hopi, and Zuni Indians to accept Catholic missionaries, in 1633.

There was a demand for livestock owned by friars at the missions. Santa Fe citizens complained to the viceroy in 1639, that the missions had too many animals; each mission owned 30 animals including cows, horses, and oxen. The Spanish government forbade trading horses to the Indians. Rosas captured Ute Indians for slaves and made many enemies. The unpopular Rosas was subsequently murdered.

The nomadic Ute Indians first made contact with the Spanish and consequently were the first American Indians to possess the horse before any other tribe. After the Ute, the Apache, Comanche, Navajo, and other nomadic Indians had horses.

In 1650, Ute Indians on horseback raided for additional horses in New Mexico, when huge amounts of wild horses ran free. The colonists allowed their horses to graze loose without corrals and ponies in the mesteño bands were easy for the Indian to steal. They began building large herds of ponies.

In the 1670's, drought and famine raged among the Puebla's; attacks were increased from neighboring nomadic tribes. As the Spaniard vacated the region, Apache and Navajo war parties increased their raids. Due to an increase of attacks, some Spanish soldiers were unable to defend the Pueblos. At the same time, European diseases ravaged the Pueblos, the death rate was high. The Pueblo Revolt did not bring peace. Although the Puebla's returned to their traditional religion, their gods did not bring rain to end the famine. The Pueblo Indians became dissatisfied with the Spanish.

The Indians turned to their old religion. The missionaries ignored the Indians performing their dances. Fray Alonso forbade the Kachina Dances of the Pueblo Indians and ordered the missionaries to seize and destroy every effigy, mask, and prayer stick that they could find. The Puebloans were forbidden to practice their native religion by the Franciscans, who were charged with heresy and tried before the Spanish Inquisition to curb their power. The Pueblo Indians had the will to unite, but lacked the means to remain united after conquering their enemies.

Refugees from the Isleta Pueblo abandoned their homes and journeyed to El Paso in September of 1670. In retaliation, the Pueblo Indians destroyed most homes and buildings of the Spanish. Spain attempted to re-conquer the Pueblos.

There was unrest among the Navajo and Pueblo Indians, who planned to drive out the Spanish. Pueblo Indian slaves to the Spanish gave colonists' horses away to the Navajo warriors. The abuse continued until around 1680, when the Indians rebelled.

In 1680, Pope, a San Juan Pueblo Indian medicine man, who was flogged and mistreated by the Spanish, led a rebellion by the Picuris, Taos, and Tewa Pueblos against the Spanish colonists. Indian tribes rose up and overthrew the Spanish rule during the "Pueblo Revolt" driving out the Spanish colonists, priests and soldiers. They killed 380 Spanish colonists, including women and children. Twenty one Franciscan priests were murdered during the insurrection. One thousand others were allowed to flee. Many Spaniards were killed. The Indians sacked the mission cathedrals and tearing them down and ended Catholic ritual. They set out to restore their old traditions.

Over 400 Spanish survivors fled to the governor's palace in Santa Fe. The Indians lay siege on the colonist occupants. The

Spanish, lacking water for days, fled when New Mexico governor Antonio de Otermin ordered a retreat to El Paso del Norte (El, Paso, Texas).

The various Pueblo leaders fought over leadership of Santa Fe. Pope, who had led the rebellion, became chief of New Mexico territory, but the role was temporary. Pope endeavored to eradicate traces of Spanish rule and declared "the God of the Christians is dead." Many villages resented Pope and thought him to be a warlord. Many Christian converts opposed his destruction of Christian relics. Although the Spanish had left, they didn't solidify and unite. After seven years of drought, the Spanish returned.

During the Pueblo Revolt hundreds of Spanish colonists fled the country in fear, and left thousands of cattle, horses and sheep behind. They were gone twelve years. Indians rounded up the remaining horses. The Spanish colonists fled in fear in order to escape for a period of twelve years leaving their property behind. After the Pueblo Revolt horses ran free on the plains. Pueblo Indians were overwhelmed by the number of horses running loose. Domestic horses strayed or broke down fences and scattered into the desert forming herds. Hundreds of Mustangs escaped from colonists' ranches and fled into the desert and into Mexico.

Spanish longhorns dwelled among the wild horse herds even before the Pueblo Rebellion. When the Spanish fled in 1680, many longhorn beeves (cattle) were left behind. Those cows were developed into massive herd during the next century.

Mutinying Indians stole 3,000 valuable horses. Bloodlines became mixed. Horses roamed free and the Indians garnered many Spanish Mustangs at that time and became horse-mounted. Another 3,000 horses ranged on the open plains. Horses that escaped during the Great Pueblo Revolt spread into the desert and across the Great Plains. Wild horses are considered intrusive, but exotic animals that reverted to the wild. Wild horses are labeled non-native by state and federal wildlife management to protect the horses, but horses may have co-evolved from the Pleistocene and modern horses.

After the Pueblo Revolt in 1680, Comanche Indian traders drove hundred of horses they had taken from the Apaches and the Spanish North to their Shoshoni brothers in what is now modern day Idaho.

The Boise River Shoshoni held trade fairs on a huge island on the Snake River, where they traded horses, furs, bows and arrows, trade beads, iron implements, and wives. There was great festivity, gambling, music, storytelling, and horse racing.

Ownership of valuable horses changed hands. Horses having belonged to the Spanish were now possessed by the American Indians. Ponies with blood lines were used to hunt buffalo and for war horses. In 1692, Pope died. At this point, Diego de Vargas returned with his army and re-conquered New Mexico for Spain after a twelve year absence. Diego de Vargas, governor of New Mexico, organized and carried out the re-conquest and re-colonization of New Spain in 1692. de Vargas persuaded 23 Pueblos to rejoin the Spanish empire. In 1694, the Spanish colonists re-occupied Santa Fe, while the Tewa and Tano Pueblos resisted. From 1700-1800's Mexico held New Mexico as her territory. In 1846, the United States claimed New Mexico as her territory. The Mexican War occurred 1846-1848, and in 1848, the Treaty of Guadalupe Hidalgo ended the Mexican-American War. In 1850, New Mexico became a territory. Santa Fe remained the capitol and on January 6, 1912, New Mexico officially became a state as part of the United States of America.

CHAPTER THREE
THE UTE GETS THE HORSE

The Ute Indians are indigenous natives of the Great Basin Region, amidst the Rocky and Sierra Nevada Mountains, that inhabited California, Colorado, Nevada, New Mexico, and Utah, bordered on the North by the Snake River and the Colorado River on the South. The Native Americans of the Great Basin shared the same culture. The desert region is made up of brush, desert, grassland, sagebrush, and some sparse woodland. Ute Indians are closely connected to the Southern Paiute and Shoshoni Indians through the Uto-Aztecan dialect. Ute means "Land of the Sun" in their language. The Ute Indians were pedestrian Indians for thousands of years, scattered across the land, and dwelt in seven bands comprised of the Capote, Mouache, Parianucs, Tabeguache, Uintah, Weeminuche and Yampa. Various Ute bands spoke the same common Numic language and shared political and social values. Tribal history was passed down from word of mouth.

It is not known when the ancestors of the Numic-speaking Ute Indians arrived in Utah, but by 1500 A.D, they had spread through parts of Colorado, New Mexico, eastern and central Utah, and Wyoming. Ute Indians raided on foot, fought over territory, and captured slaves. They were semi-nomadic "Hunters and Gatherers" hunting beaver, bighorn, rabbits, wild turkeys and other game. Women gathered berries, nuts, and seeds. Winters were best spent in stream valleys protected from the wind; in summer the women picked berries in the mountains. They were of the Great Basin and Plains culture.

The Ute had an early history with the Spanish, pre-dating the Pueblos by a half century, the first American Indians to contact the Spanish. When Ute Indians first saw the Spanish explorers,

Ute War Party
Eminent Domain

they saw horses for the first time and thought the animals to be big dogs. Soon, the Ute Indians would have horses. They were horsed early, the first Indian tribe to have horses in America. Ute Indians had horses even before contact with white explorers. The horse revolutionized the life way of the Ute tribe. They used the buffalo horse to reach the herds, where other hunters gathered.

The semi-nomadic Ute Indians became fully nomadic with horses as Plains Indians, hunted buffalo and ranged farther roaming onto the Plains to hunt buffalo on horseback and Ute scouts located the site of a herd. As the hunt began, braves rode along-side a fleeing bison and fired their arrows killing the buffalo. Bison were skinned, gutted and jerked; then, meat and skins were loaded on pack-mules that Indians brought behind their horses for the trip back to their base-camp. Hides were scraped, treated and sewn together by the women, to be used for tipi walls. Eastern Ute Indians had the horse and lodged in tipis, while the Western Ute dwelled in wickiups.

The Ute Indians made both men's and women's wooden saddles and covered them with skins. Many warriors rode bareback. Leather from the animal hides was crafted into dresses, breech-clouts, war shirts, leggings and moccasins. Skins covered their knife sheaths, tom-toms, or were crafted into dolls, etcetera. The Ute used antelope, buffalo, deer, elk, and moose skins for their utility. With the horse, the Great Basin Ute Indians became like Plains Indians. The horse enabled the whole camp to follow the buffalo. The hunter warrior could kill enough buffalo to feed his extended family for weeks.

Comanche braves delighted in riding after Ute horsemen hunting buffalo on the plains to scare them off and scattered their camps for the sake of mischief. The Indian agent requested protection from enemy Indians. The Ute and Navajo continued to war.

Ute Indian Band
Photo Courtesy of Legend of America

In the 1500's Francisco Cortez imprisoned the Ute for stealing horses and forced them to work in the gold and silver mines. The Spanish imported horses from Europe for their Army, and Catholic missions, but most of the horses went to the colonists.

Ute Indians had been exposed to the Spanish horse culture as slaves. Ute boys were trained to herd Spanish horses. A Ute chief became familiar with horses as a herder for the Spanish over lords and learned to make bridles, saddles and other tack.

Young braves learned tricks on horseback, like leaning down picking up a bandana on the ground while in the saddle. Their horses were agile and a brave could lean down and swing a comrade up onto his horse behind him in battle. Warriors made a loop that slipped over the horse's head. A brave leaned over beneath its head and could shoot or dodge arrows in battle at a full gallop.

In 1598, New Mexico was settled by the Spanish. Over time, the Spanish established trade with the Ute people, although it was prohibited by the government. Owning horses increased Ute raids and the number of prisoners. The Mouache Ute traded a few horses from the Spanish in 1580.

In 1626, the earliest written record of the Ute Indians was notated by the Spanish. War parties raided on horseback to steal additional horses, a form of counting coup and going on the war trail for ponies. The Ute gained horses on night raids from the Spanish colonists until the mid 1600's.

Around 1650, the Ute quit stealing horses from the Spanish and instead began to trade with the Spanish colonists and the Ute Indians entered into the slave trade with the Spanish colonists trading Indian slaves for horses. With horses, their whole mode of fighting radically changed. On horseback, the Ute warriors went on the warpath by the light of the moon riding into unsuspecting

41

villages, defeating the enemy, and capturing Indian women and children for slaves.

Ute Indians raided the Hopi, Navajo, Paiute, and Shoshoni Indians on horseback trading slaves they had captured to the Spanish, for horses. The colonists used the slaves in their households. Girls were trained as housekeepers and boys cared for the colonists' cattle and sheep. Ute Indians had a notorious slave trade with the Spanish.

In 1670, the first peace treaty was written between the Ute and the Spanish. In 1676, Escalante conducted an expedition through Ute territory. The Spanish bartered beads, pottery, and grain for buffalo meat and hides from the Indians. The Spanish enjoyed the opportunity of trading with the Indians.

In 1680, Pueblo Indians that had been enslaved by the Spanish rose up in rebellion and overthrew the Spanish rule. They fled from New Mexico for twelve years. In 1680, during the Pueblo Revolt, the Pueblos drove the Spanish out of the country. Horses busted out of their stalls and ran loose. Soon after, the Apache and Comanche had horses.

Plains Indians had the horse as early as 1700 A.D., which altered the Plains culture. For the next 175 years Indians had horses during the "Horse and Indian Era." Walking Indians became fully nomadic; hunting was extended. Possessing horses was a status symbol of wealth. They captured more horses, their sole means of travel. The "Horse and Buffalo Era" was good for them. Hunter and horse had a special bond. In warfare, a good horse could mean the difference between life and death especially after training and becoming accustomed to gunfire. The horse had to respond to his master's commands. Training the horse for hunting and for war meant the difference between life and death for the horse-warrior. Horses were trained to withstand loud gunfire and to respond to their commands and be agile. Warriors shared battle honors with their horses and painted them with war paint, sharing symbols of war. They trimmed their horse's manes and tails and adorned them with eagle feathers and scalp locks.

The Spanish campaign to prevent raids by the Comanche and Ute failed. The Ute continued to raid New Mexico settlements from 1730-1750.

Nomadic Indians traded for horses from the Apache, Comanche, and Ute Indians, who were excellent riders having gotten the horse early. Apache, Comanche and Ute Indian tribes, horses were diffused onto the Northern Plains.

The real horse brokers, who drove the most ponies north, were the Comanche tribe. The Comanche loved their horses and were superior riders. Horse complexes in the North were centers where Indian ponies were traded to the surrounding tribes. The Cheyenne, Mandan and Shoshoni were examples.

Early hunting paths became trails to move horses northward and were used as trade routes for the Indians. One trade route led from the Spanish colonies and the Indian Pueblos of New Mexico northward to the Black Hills in South Dakota reaching the Arikara, and Hidatsa. Another major trade center in which to barter was the Mandan Indian trade center, a special hub for the Indian horse trade. The other route led from the Upper Yellowstone eastward where horses were trailed. In 1746, the Spanish defeated the Comanche and Ute Indian allies near Abiquiui. In 1779, Ute and Jicarilla Apache Indians joined in alliance with Anza against the Comanche tribe.

Ute Indians drove the Navajo people from the San Juan River drainage. Ute Indian chiefs Moara and Pinto protested against the Comanche Indian and Spanish peace treaty in 1786. Juan de Anza wrote a peace with the Comanche, Spanish and Ute

Ute Chief Ignacio & Indian pony
Eminent Domain

44

Indians. In 1789, another treaty was written with the Ute and Spanish against the Comanche and Navajo Indians.

The Spanish did not trust the Indians of the Plains and sent Ute Indian spies to gather information about the Plains Indians in 1801. In 1804, the Apache and Ute joined the Spanish in a campaign against the Navajo Indians.

The Spanish pitted the various Indian tribes against each other in order to defeat them. The Spanish wrote treaties among the tribes, but the Ute and Navajo Indians still continued to war against each other. Later, the Ute and Navajo Indians conjoined and fought the Hopi Indians, while the Spanish continued their fight against the Comanche Indians.

In 1806, 400 Mouache Ute warriors battled an equal number of Comanche Indians near Taos. Lt. Zebulon Pike passed through Ute territory at nearly the same time, the first Euro-American to explore the region using Ute Indians scouts. In 1809, 600 Mouache Ute and some Jicarilla Apache braves were attacked by Comanche, Cuampe and Kiowa Indians. Ute chiefs Delgadito, El Alba, and Mano Mocha, were killed.

Comanche Indians fought the Ute warriors for more than 100 years. In 1829, the Old Spanish Trail was opened partly through Ute territory. Old Bent's Fort was opened in 1832 in Ute territory. The Old Spanish Trail was passage for the Ute Indians from the Great Plains to California. The Old Ute Trail was used by the Arapaho and Ute Indians on their way between their winter and summer hunting grounds. There was much game along the trail: buffalo, elk, moose, mountain goats, and sheep.

In the 1840's, the Ute war parties were constantly attacking the white settlements of New Mexico. Then in 1844, Ute warriors attacked the governor of New Mexico's office in Santa Fe. The Ute had to be brought to the peace table.

In 1846, Colonel Donovan reached a peace agreement with 60 Ute Indians and in 1849, the first peace treaty between the United States and the Ute Indians was signed in Abiquiu. Principal Ute Chief Quiziachigiate and 28 sub-chiefs signed. In 1850, the Ute obtained arms from the Mormons. They continued to fight the Kiowa and Arapaho.

An Indian agency was opened for the Ute Indians in Taos, New Mexico then closed down. The agency reopened and was run by Agent Christopher "Kit" Carson from 1853-1859. The Ute Indians fought over the game along the Arkansas River.

The Uintah and Ouray Indian Reservation were established in 1861 by executive order. The Uintah Valley was set aside for the San Juan County, New Mexico and San Juan County, Utah tribal industry, which includes agriculture, forestry, and mineral resources. The reservation lies in northeastern Utah.

There are three Ute reservations in Utah: the Uintah-Ouray, the Southern Ute, and the Ute Mountain. The Ute Mountain Reservation covers nearly 600,000 acres of allotted and deeded lands primarily in Colorado extending into New Mexico and Utah. The reservation was inhabited by the year 2,000 northern with Ute members, mostly from the Mountain Ute Tribe.

The tribe benefits from various gas, oil, and mineral deposits on the reserve. The Mountain Ute Reservation surrounds the Mesa Verde National Park on three sides. Total land area is 6719.173 square miles, population 19,182 members, joined by the White River Band.

In 1868, a huge reservation was established for the Southern Ute Indians over 56 million acres, until gold was discovered in the mountains, so the government diminished the Ute Indians' land. The Ute people lost their hunting grounds, where deer and elk were hunted.

The Southern Ute Indian Reservation was established in 1895 in the southwestern corner of Colorado and covers approximately 300,000 acres, crossing 7 rivers, featuring mountainous timber acres to the east and flat land to the west. There are over 1400 tribal members. The Ute bands, who originally resided there were the Capote, Muache, and Weeminuche that comprised the Southern Ute Indians. The tribe has a Tribal Council of 7 members and a Constitution. The Ute Indian tribe develops gas, gravel, oil, and sand enrichments.

The traditional Southern Ute Bear Dance and Feast is celebrated when the bears emergence from hibernation. The traditional Ute Sun Dance is performed during the second weekend in July.

The Southern Ute Fair and Powwow is held on the second weekend in September. Activities are arts and crafts display sales, dances, food, games and the Powwow. Other activities are Sky Ute Bingo, Lake Capote, Navajo State Park and Ute Memorial Park.

Ute Memorial Park was established in order to preserve the prehistoric culture of the Ancient Indians known as Anasazi. The "Ancient Ones" are thought to be ancestors of the modern Pueblo Indians. The ancestral Pueblo people were a prehistoric Native American civilization. They inhabited the Four Corners country of Southern Utah, southwestern Colorado, northwestern New Mexico, and northern Arizona from about A.D. 200 to A.D. 1300, leaving their Pueblo house remains and debris.

The Anasazi Indians also credited for the fascinating cliff pueblos found throughout the Four Corners area of what is now Arizona, New Mexico, Colorado and Utah. The name Anasazi comes from the Navajo Indians loosely translated enemy ancestors. Hopi Indians claim that the Anasazi Indians were their ancestors.

Ute Indians Had the First Horses
Photo Courtesy of Azusa Publishing, LLC

Ute Horsemen Petroglyphs
Photo Courtesy of Wikipedia.org

CHAPTER FOUR
WILD MUSTANGS

Ancient horses became extinct thousands of years ago. Berbers that conquered Spain rode the finest Arabians that descended from Arab-Turkic origins. Not until the Spanish brought horses in their sailing ships (galleons) did horses reappear on America's horizon. Strains of blue-bloods were bred from Arabian horses from Spain. Many horses escaped from the conquistadors and entered the wild and became Mustangs in the canyons, mountains and plains. Barb-Arab horses (Barbs) were fine ponies. Some retained the strong characteristics of Spanish decent. Breeders of domestic horses thought wild herds to be of inferior quality due to inbreeding, but that may not have been the case. Spanish Mustangs have changed due to inbreeding. Others show mixed blood because of ranch breeding.

In the West wild horses roamed free on the desert of the Southern Plains. The Pueblo Indians drove the Spanish out and horses escaped. Feral horses were domesticated horses that escaped during the Pueblo Revolt and reverted back to the wild. Herds multiplied from several dozen horses numbering into the millions in 150 years. Their defense in the wild was their hooves and speed and ranged from the Mississippi west to the California coast, living symbols of the pioneer spirit of the American West.

The word, Mustang comes from the Spanish word mesteño meaning stray livestock animal. "Small herds or "wild bunches" expanded into larger ones. Millions of horses ran free in the deserts of the Great Basin, Great Plains, and California's San Joaquin Valley.

Mustangs had short backs, smooth muscles, rounded rumps, set tails, and dorsal stripes from mane to tail, which were long and dark, with a colored fringe. Forelegs had tiger striped

49

Mustang Mare and Foal
Photo Courtesy of Wikipedia.org

Free-roaming wild horse herd in Utah in 2005
Photo Courtesy of Wikipedia.org

markings. Legs were short and stocky; they had a mule hoof. A popular term describing the southwestern desert was "Mustang Country," where free-roaming horses and burros ran loose.

Indians received horses by theft, strays, or from wild herds and adapted to them quickly. They highly prized wild horses and rarely parted with them. Catlin said the Mandan Indians could throw a lariat from a Mustang riding at full speed and lasso the wild horse. Horses from range herds scattered across the desert.

A Pawnee Indian told the saga of an Indian who roped a Mustang that was so frightened it jerked his captor's horse down and crushed the rider. The Pawnee bordered the Comanche and were able to trade for or steal horses from them, counting coup.

The Alpha-male led the herd and bred all of the mares. As pregnant mares reproduced the herds grew in size. Over a ten year period the herd doubled. Colts accompanied their mothers. Herds spread across the desert. Wild horses gathered on the plains by the thousands and into the millions.

The stud closely guarded his mares and was known to stampede his herd through a domestic herd to steal mares. A stallion might lead a large herd of 200-300 mares. A wild horse herd led by a raging alpha stallion could steal a bunch of domestic horses and lead them off. In addition to horses, pack mules broke free and escaped. There were jack-ass and she-ass herds roaming in small desert herds.

Ranchers shot Alpha-male stallions as "outlaws" and replacing them with pedigreed stallions to improve the wild herds. Since the 1700's, wild horses were referred to as Mustangs.

Using the relay method, a rider pursued the ponies until his horse was winded and then another cowpoke took up the chase until the herd began to tire out and was caught. The circling method involved surrounding and lassoing the horses.

Feral Horses in Nevada Desert
Photo Courtesy of Wikipedia.org

Free-Roaming Wild Spanish Mustangs in the Desert
Photo Courtesy of Wikipedia.org

Life in the desert was hard on the wild horses. Wild free-roaming Mustangs had to adapt to blizzards, disease, drought, lightning, predators rattlesnakes and harsh weather. Wild bunches found it difficult to find grass in snowy regions; they drifted from one exposed dry grass patch to the next. In a similar way, buffalo scraped snow off grass with their horns. Some feral horses had stunted growth from enduring harsh winters on the plains.

The finest bred horses now mated by natural selection. The wild bunch exhibits that breeds became intermixed and may have been introduced to a domestic stud by breeders. A wild bunch may be all the same color. Ranchers released their horses to forage and survive in the winter and then recaptured the horses in the spring.

Spanish stock supplied the early ranches in America. Wild horses made good saddle broncos. Horse's lived twenty eight years or longer. Wild horses were highly prized; horses caught in the wild were worth money if broken to ride first.

Paint Horses are descendants of horses brought from Spain by Conquistadors that joined the free-roaming wild bunch on the western plains. If a Pinto and a western stock horse mated the foal was a called a Paint, which seems to have larger blotches of color. The American Paint horse was loved by the cowboys and ranch workers and was a good horse to ride.

The Paint Horse and the Pinto Horse were favorite mounts of the American Indians. Indians caught and rode the beautiful Paint Horse believing the colored pony to be magical. They believed that these horses were from the spiritual world and had magical powers and could empower their masters who rode them.

North Africa Barbs and the medieval Andalusia Horses were bred into Spanish Jennets and Sorraia Horses. American bred horses tracing from the Dutch, English, French, Irish and other bloodlines were mixed with Spanish Mustangs.

Wild Horses in the Desert
Photo Courtesy of Wikipedia.org

Mare and Foal Get a Cool Drink
Photo Courtesy of Wikipedia.org

The land between the Nueces and the Rio Grande was called the "Wild Horse Desert" because of its huge herds of wild horses (Mustangs or Mesteños). The herds were a wondrous sight. There were wild horse herds in northern Mexico that must have drifted across the Rio Grande and into the Wild Horse Desert.

Accounts say the wild horses were the offspring of Mustangs that strayed from the conquistadors in the 17th century or the strays had been left because they had become lame and could not continue. The open grasslands of Southern Texas extended across the coastal plains and into Mexico. The descendents of Spanish horses flourished on the plains.

The governor of Coahuila in 1735 observed massive herds of horses that had once been domesticated and had escaped and become wild. Jose Escandon established settlements on South Texas and along the Rio Grande and discovered wild horses in 1747. In 1768, on a mission tour of Texas, Fray Gaspar Jose de Solis found wild horses around Laredo. Father Juan Agustin Morfi espied wild horse herds in 1777 north of the Rio Grande, where horse trails cut deep into the landscape.

In 1828, Manuel de Mier observed great herds of wild horses below Nueces, where one had to keep sentries to prevent mules and packhorses from running off with the wild bunch. Wild herds were prevalent in the Wild Horse Desert in 1845, when Zachary Taylor's army was encamped in Corpus Christi.

A story was told how young Second Lieutenant Ulysses S. Grant had purchased four Mustang ponies for a few dollars a head. His hired man lost them when he took them down to get a drink. Taylor's adjutant joked, "I heard that Grant lost five or six dollars worth of horses." Grant remarked that it was slander and that the horses were worth $20.00. Grant went out to see the great herds of horses and thought them too many to be contained in Rhode Island.

55

Wild Stallions Fighting
Photo Courtesy of Wikipedia.org

Wild Horses in Pryor Mountain Range
Photo Courtesy of Wikipedia.org

One operation was for cowboys to catch wild cattle for resale. Another occupation was to hunt wild horses. Hunting wild Mustangs in 1848 was big business. Mustangers went to work capturing the magnificent beasts. Mustangs were caught and tamed. Others were sold to be slaughtered and skinned, the hides salted down and sold in New Orleans. Thousands of ponies were shipped from Topeka west to range country. In 1884, thousands of horses were shipped out West.

Some of the horses were broken to the saddle and sold. A rather cruel method of catching a prize Mustang was by creasing. Creasing was to use a rifle and shoot the animal close to the spinal cord in order to subdue it. A missed shot proved fatal to the horse. A captain of a Mustang crew described his method of capturing wild Mustangs. The procedure was nearly identical to the method used by the American Indians to capture antelope.

The trap was a pen with wings built in a v of brush that ran into the opening. The Mustangs were driven down the corridor into the gap by the cowboys. A cowboy waved a white blanket to keep the horses in. As the Mustangs entered the pen, the gate was closed behind the horses. Confused, the Mustangs circled inside the pen.

With bands of horses as large as buffalo herds, wild horses were caught by the dozens and sold for individual use, ranches, and use by the Army. A single horse sold for $8.00-$12.00 or were sometimes wholesaled for as low $36.00 per dozen.

They told of Army officers selecting wild horses with heavy manes and tales for their own use, referring to the Spanish Mustangs. Attempting to corral too many wild horses resulted in injury and sometimes death among the Mustangs. Hunting horses was so extensive that the wild bunch started vanishing, like the buffalo into extinction. Wild herds in the desert were picturesque and the spirit of America.

Wild Horses Grazing
Photo Courtesy of Wikipedia.org

There are numerous accounts in diaries and journals from the mid-1800s of massive herds of Spanish Mustangs, but the numbers were left out. It has been estimated that there were a million horses on the Texas Plains, alone. That count could be increased to many millions more by adding the wild bunches in the Great Basin, the Great Plains, and the northern Plateau regions.

Wild horse herds in the "Mustang Desert" grew on a steady basis. Free roaming stallions stole mares from Indians, settlers, and different herds. Stallions governed the size of their herds. Steeds could draw out females using their deep throat neighs and tender whinnies in order to build their own herds. A wild bunch could double in size over a ten year period.

Pioneers traveling along the Oregon Trail traded with the Cayuse Indian tribe for their famous ponies. Settlers began to refer to these Indian ponies in slang as "Ole Cayuses." The Cayuse pony was a good, sturdy bred to own.

After the 1862 Homestead Act, many farmers acquired 160 acre homesteads and waited the required 5 years to finalize. They found a need for horses. Hundreds of Europeans immigrated to America to acquire land. Thousands of settlers moved west to get their homesteads.

Today, wild horses still range loose in the desert roaming free and the largest number of feral horses roams in the state of Nevada. It is a marvelous sight to see a gorgeous herd of wild horses spook and suddenly stampede when frightened.

In 2007 in Browning, Montana, and Bob "Black Bull" Bedard in his search for Spanish Mustangs with an interest in the native's horse culture created the Blackfeet Buffalo Horse Coalition. The society in the 1.5 million acre Glacier National Park was created to shelter Spanish Mustangs and teach children about horses.

1800's Comanche Warrior
Photo Courtesy of Wikipedia.org

Comanche Indians on Horseback
Photo Courtesy of Wikipedia.com

CHAPTER FIVE
COMANCHE TRADERS

Prehistoric ancestors of the Comanche crossed the Bering Straits over the land bridge and entered Alaska, Canada and America, thousands of years ago. Early on, the Northern Shoshoni tribes were "Walking Shoshonis" and traveled everywhere on foot. Legend tells us that five bands of Shoshoni Indians split from the Eastern Shoshoni tribe at Wind River, Wyoming tribe and migrated south.

Stories have been passed down over time to explain how the Comanche-Shoshoni division occurred. One tale from legend told of how two bands of Shoshoni Indians joined together in a hunting party and killed a bear. An argument arose over whose arrow killed the bruin and how to divide it. A brave from each band claimed the victory. Then, one of the bands moved away. Another account told how they departed from the Eastern Shoshoni. A band of Shoshoni traveling south was startled by the eerie howl of a timber wolf nearby. Some in the party counted the wolf cry as a bad omen. The chief and half of the band turned back. The rest of the band chose a new head man and continued to migrate southward and become Comanche Indians.

Bands that split off had migrated south, left the Shoshoni Indian territory circa 1500 A. D., moved across Colorado, Nebraska, Kansas, and Oklahoma. Continuing south, they chose the region, known as northern Texas to lodge and settled around the headwaters of the Brazos, Cimarron, Canadian and Red Rivers. Historical record placed Comanche Indians in New Mexico early in the 16th Century, the Shoshoni Indians of the Southern Plains.

The name "Comanche" is from the Ute name for them, Kohmahts (one who wants to fight me all of the time, or enemy). The Spanish and U.S. Armies called them the Comanche Indians.

Fearless warriors fought anyone in their path, including enemy tribes, Mexican Armies, Spanish Armies and Texas Rangers and the U.S. Army preventing Spanish expansion in Texas.

When they migrated to northern Texas, they impacted the Jicarilla Apache Indians, who were peaceful buffalo hunters and farmers that had learned agriculture from the Pueblo Indians. The Apaches stayed in one location growing beans, corn and squash. Living near the Spanish, they began to steal horses.

Comanche men wore animal skin shirts, skin loin cloths and leather boots. They adorned their hair with feathers or a buffalo scalp with horns for headgear in battle.

Apaches had the horse early and raided the Spanish colonists for horses in the 1600's and like the Comanche, Apache mythology regarded the horse as a gift from the gods to man for his use. They believed various colored horses represented a piece of the sky. White ponies were special to Apaches and were used for hunting and war. During the 1600's, the Apache built large herds. Comanche favored War Bonnet Horses with color atop their heads, ears and on the chest. These horses were considered sacred.

As the Comanche acquired horses from the Apaches, they became even bolder in battle. The Comanche frightened their enemies and terrorized the settlers. The fierce Comanche forced the Apache, Tonka and Wichita peoples from the Southern Plains.

In the summer, the Comanche went on night raids by the light of a full moon raiding so often that the term, "Comanche Moon" was used and is still applied in Texas, today. They slipped away at night and stole horses under the Comanche Moon from the Apache, an act of bravery, and a way of counting coup. Comanche braves did not consider stealing horses theft; they believed that the "great spirit" had given them the horse and it was especially theirs. They went out on small raiding parties and took what was theirs.

War Chief Quanah Parker on His Favorite Horse
Photo Courtesy of Wikipedia.org

War parties of two or three dozen braves prided themselves in the art of slipping into an enemy camp at night, cutting the hobbles of an Indian pony, and stealing it without awakening the camp.

More horses were taken after the Pueblo Revolt. Comanche Indians acquired more horses around 1680 having stolen horses early from the Apaches, when thousands of wild horses that had broken out roamed the desert. They regarded the horse as a gift from the gods and cherished horses becoming legendary horsemen.

The Comanche caught wild horses. The wild stallion was a powerful runner and could sometimes outdistance a pursuer or lead a wild herd. Comanche Indians used lassos to catch wild Mustangs, a method learned from the Spanish. They could approach a feral horse and encircle its head with a lasso in the wild. When Comanche braves caught a mare with its foal, the mother slowed down and stayed with her colt, thus catching two horses.

The Comanche horsemen captured Mustangs best in the winter, when they were undernourished and too weak to resist and escape. In cold weather, wild horses were weaker, gaunter and starving. They had less resistance and were easier to catch.

The Comanche children were gifted ponies and learned to ride as youngsters; they spent hours racing their ponies. As young braves, they performed tricks vaulting onto their horses from the rear and could lean down from a moving horse and pick up a neckerchief.

On a galloping pony they learned to shift to one side down low and fire arrows under their horses' necks. An arrow could kill a man or a horse. They became the most expert horsemen and the fiercest warriors. Men, women and children all rode horses.

If a brave loved an Indian maiden and desired to wed her, he left a string of around 25 ponies tied to her teepee. Such a practice was called bride price. If she accepted the gift, they were soon wed.

**Indians used mules to pack buffalo meat and robes back to camp.
Author Photo**

In 1692, an Apache, Hopi, and Paiute alliance was made to counter Spanish aggression. Anza's peace agreement allowed freedom of movement and free trade. In 1700, Apache, Comanche and Ute Indians raided the Pueblos and Spanish colonists. After the Pueblo Revolt in 1680, the Comanche had a huge surplus of horses.

Legend tells how the Comanche drove possibly, 2,000 head of horses north circa 1700 A.D. to trade to their Northern Shoshoni cousins, indicating their point of origin and the Comanche's very beginnings. Horse brokers, the Comanche Indians went on to provide horses to most of the Indian tribes in the Pacific Northwest and the Central Plains.

The Comanche traded horses to the Northern Shoshoni Indians who hosted trade fairs. From there, horses diffused to the various tribes of the Northwest. The horse was well distributed by the Comanche Indians to the tribes on the Northern Plains. Horses fanned over the Pacific Northwest and eastward over the Central Plains, reaching the Northeast. The Comanche tribe became a "horse nation." They were fully horsed by 1720 A.D.

The first time that the Cayuse ever saw horses was when they saw a Comanche band riding strange mane animals, called "kawas." The first raids by Comanche braves were recorded in New Mexico, from 1714-1720. In 1716, the Spanish Army launched a campaign against the Comanche and Ute.

In 1776, Governor Juan Baptiste de Anza signed a treaty with the Plains Indians allowing trade between New Mexico and the Indians. In return, the Comanche were to be peaceable toward the Spaniards in Texas. This began a long lasting alliance.

Comanche traded with the French traders and traded many horses to white men. The Comanche language became a trade language with other tribes in the southwest.

War Chief Quanah Parker
Photo Courtesy of Legends of America

Captain Randolph Marcy proclaimed the Comanche Indians to be the most expert horsemen in the world. George Catlin corroborated views. "In racing and riding," Catlin agreed, "they are not equaled by any other Indians on the continent."

Comanche Indians continued to raid for horses, as did the Apache, Navajo, and Ute Indians, who stormed Spanish Colonists' ranchos. Becoming horse-mounted, the Comanche raided the Spanish haciendas of Mexican colonists in New Mexico, Texas and Mexico stealing Mustangs from their rancheros.

Comanche thought horses were there for the taking and amassed thousands of mustangs. Wealth in horses came in the number owned; the Comanche Indians amassed large herds. It was not uncommon for a warrior to own 250 horses. A chief could possess a herd of 1,000.

Horses were gifted, traded, stolen or caught wild. Horses changed their life way, warfare, hunting, camp and seasonal moves. They became Horse and Buffalo Indians.

The Comanche did not practice selective breeding like the Nez Perce with their Appaloosa horse, but picked characteristics like color, size and swiftness.

The Nez Perce Indians received the Appaloosa horse from the Comanche horsemen; the beautiful Appaloosa horse with the spotted rump became their favorite breed. The Jennet horse is the predecessor of the Appaloosa. Although the Nez Perce are attributed with developing the Appaloosa horse, their neighbors, the Palouse Indians did also. Both tribes favored the spotted horse and bred them.

The Nez Perce and Palouse were allies and spoke the same language. The name, "Appaloosa" came from French fur trappers for horses owned by the Palouse tribe. In French, Palouse meant "the green hills," where the tribe lived.

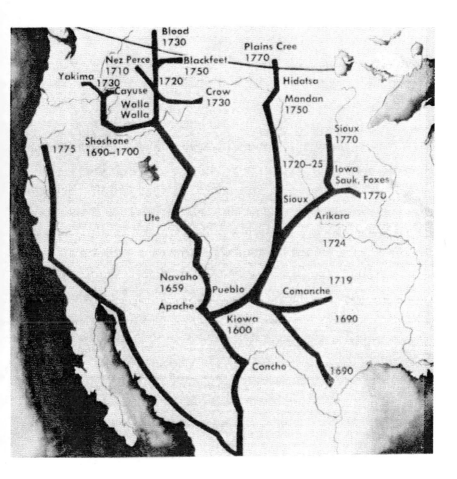

Blood
1730

Nez Perce
1710

Blackfeet
1750

Plains Cree
1770

Yakima
1730

Cayuse
Walla
Walla

1720

Crow
1730

Hidatsa

Mandan
1750

Shoshone
1690–1700

1775

Sioux
1770

1720–25

Iowa
Sauk, Foxes

1770

Ute

Sioux

Arikara

1724

Navaho
1659

Pueblo

Comanche

1719

Apache

1690

Kiowa
1600

Concho

1690

Comanche Trailed Horses North after the Pueblo Revolt.
Eminent Domain

69

Comanche Indians traded horses to the Blackfeet, Cayuse, Crow, and Walla-Walla Indians. Trade routes extended north to the Hidatsa, Mandan and Sioux and crisscrossed the northwest; horses reached Indians by diffusion. Cheyenne, Crow, and Mandan tribes had trade centers for horses. Possibly, hunting trails were used to drive herds of horses north.

Plains Indians raided horses from enemy camps and took slaves of women and children. It has been estimated that the Comanche captured over 20,000 Caucasian, Chinese, Mexican, and Indian captives over a 150 year period and traded slaves for horses at trade fairs in Taos, the Pueblos and Santa Fe.

The Comanche bartered buffalo hides and horses to the reservation and conducted festive trade fair celebrations. The pipe was smoked; there was song, dance and storytelling. Gambling and horse racing were favorites. The Comanche traded buffalo robes, horses, bows and arrows, knives and wives. The Comanche dialect became a trade language with the other tribes.

Around 700 families settled in Texas shortly after the Mexican War of Independence from Spain, but there was no regular army to protect the citizens. The Texas Rangers were the second oldest law enforcement agency in the state of Texas. The horse-mounted Texas Rangers were initiated as a group in 1823, two years after white settlement began. Stephen Austin organized some experienced frontiersmen as rangers in informal groups to protect the settlers against Indian war parties attacking ranches, and other criminal elements. It was on November 24, 1835, that Austin organized the Texas Rangers.

Nelson Lee was one of three Texas Rangers taken captive by the Comanche. He survived as a slave only because he possessed a pocket watch which played a song. The Comanche thought that he was a medicine man. Lee described this scenario:

'On one occasion when traveling to another village, the Indians happened onto a black bear. One horseman lassoed the bear's head, while another roped his back leg. Comanche horses backed up, stretching the bear, as one warrior cut its throat. They cooked the bear for supper, much like in a modern rodeo.'

When Sam Houston was selected to the presidency in 1841, he saw the usefulness of the Rangers. On January 25, 1841, he approved a law which provided a company of mounted men to act as Rangers. Captain "Jack" Coffee Hays and 150 men were assigned to protect the Lone Star State. In 1846, the United States declared war on Mexico. In the war, the Rangers, known as the "Texas Devils," fought the Mexican guerillas.

In 1845, Quanah was born in a tipi in the Wichita Mountains, to a Comanche chief and a white captive woman, Cynthia Parker. Quanah received his spirit guide, counted coup and become a tall strong brave. He killed an enemy warrior at 15 on a raid. Quanah would become the greatest chief of the Comanche tribe.

The Comanche fought the palefaces for 150 years. In 1860, Chief Quanah led the Comanche, Kiowa, Kiowa-Apache and Southern Plains Arapaho against the white-eyes. Quanah rode proudly on his black stallion, at the head of a band of several hundred whooping Indian warriors. The U.S. Army sent three columns of troops to fight the Comanche and Kiowa Indians, who had closed the Santa Fe Trail.

During the war on the Southern Plains, marauding Comanche and Kiowa war parties made vicious raids on white settlements. Quanah and his band were relentless in their attacks.

The first Battle of Adobe Walls occurred on November 25, 1864, when Colonel Christopher Houston Carson engaged the Comanche, Kiowa and Kiowa-Apache in war. Colonel "Kit"

Carson headed the march toward Adobe Walls and a winter camp of Comanche and Kiowa Indians on the Texas panhandle, where Kit had worked at Bent's Fort 20 years earlier. His scouts saw a large body of Indians, horses and cattle mingling around Adobe Walls. The men were ordered to remain silent on November 25. At around 8:30 a.m., Carson's men attacked Chief Dohasan's village of about 150 lodges and routed them.

Rations were running low and Colonel Carson called a retreat; his men were outnumbered by several thousand Indians. The Comanche braves realized this and started brush fires burning toward them to block their retreat. Carson continued rifle fire and countered by moving to higher ground and starting fires, also. Kit gave the order to burn the Comanche, Kiowa, and Kiowa-Apache lodges. The Army torched the teepees. Kiowa Chief Iron Shirt refused to leave his dwelling and died in the fire. Robes, weapons and rations were destroyed.

Colonel Kit Carson continued his retreat. Low on supplies, he reconnoitered with Lieutenant Colonel Abreau's column, coming from Mule Springs. The two forces united and camped for the night. The next day they rode to Fort Bascom and disbanded. In four days Colonel Carson had won a great victory. The Indians lost 150 warriors and 175 lodges; Carson's losses were three dead, 25 wounded, and three more died later.

During the Treaty of Little Arkansas in 1865, the Comanche tribe was awarded a large tract of land spanning parts of Oklahoma and Texas called Comancheria. New Mexico was a trade Mecca, Santa Fe being its center.

Mexican traders had the freedom to travel in Comanche territory over much of Colorado, Kansas, New Mexico, Oklahoma, and Texas. Mexican merchants moved freely across the border to trade goods with the Comanche Indians. They

Comanche Chief Quanah Parker
Public Domain

maintained their territory, keeping strangers out and guarding it like a dynasty. Expert horsemen and fierce warriors, they were truly Lords of the Plains. They painted their horses for war. A rump handprint on a horse signified a trusty horse that brought his master home safely from battle. The fierce Comanche Indians ruled the Southern Plains.

Mexican traders crossed into the United States and brought wonderful treasures from Spain for trade, including guns, glass beads and colorful pottery. The Spanish Army named them, "Comancheros." The U.S. Army also used the term.

They ranged over a large area, from the Wichita Mountains of Oklahoma, southeast to the Davis Mountains in Texas north to the Dakotas. Their center of trade was the Llano Estacado and Palo Duro Canyon in Comanche country.

The Spanish traders first brought goods into the country by pack-mule and later hauled their goods by oxen-drawn carts (carretas) to the Indian villages along old Indian trails that cut deep ruts in the prairie. T h e y were nomadic Hispanic traders in north central New Mexico Territory, who traded with the Indians.

Horses were important to the Comanche. The advent of the horse revolutionized the Plains life way. Horses were their whole life. Having a good buffalo and war horse was a given. Comanche "Horse Culture" was widespread among the tribe. Every band possessed horses. Children were raised on horses.

One method of the Indian gentling method of breaking horses was unique. Four men held the horse's lariat, while a fifth worked the horse grunting in low tones as he walked up to the Mustang, waved a blanket and hissed at the horse, mesmerizing him. Soon, he stroked the horse's head. The Indian slipped the halter over its head and again, hissed, rubbed its head, neck and flank. A blanket was brushed up against one side, then the other. The horse whisperer threw the blanket over the horse's back.

He then mounted and rode the horse. The Comanche were excellent horse handlers. Pack horses were broken in for hauling loads using rocks to represent weight they would be carrying. That way, they were conditioned to carry heavy loads.

Lassoes (Lariats) were made from buffalo hides. The use of the lasso, normally strips of leather twenty feet long and two fingers wide, was learned from the Spanish. Other ropes were made of braided animal hair. Indians braided the hair from the mane and tail of horses and the forelock of the buffalo into ropes and made stuffed dolls, and pillows of animal hair. Indian Saddles were crafted for men and women. Indian women were proficient horsewomen also. The Comanche Indians hunted on horseback.

When a medicine man predicted that a bison herd was near, scouts located the herd. Hunters on horseback were readied and the hunt was on. The headman gave a shout. Startled, the buffalo stampeded and a brave raced alongside one. He fired his arrows between its ribs to kill the beast as it stumbled and died. Comanche were skilled hunters. The buffalo were cleaned and dressed out. The meat was jerked. The jerky and hides were loaded on pack-mules for the journey back to the village.

Adobe Walls, in the Texas panhandle, was an abandoned fort used by buffalo hunters as their rendezvous headquarters and led by Col. Ranald McKenzie, a famous Indian fighter.

Quanah had petitioned the chiefs of the Arapaho, Kiowa and Southern Cheyenne tribes to smoke the pipe to war on the whites and avenge the death of an old friend at the hands of the troops and their Tonkawa Indian scouts. So on June 27, 1874, Chief Quanah Parker formed his war party of 700 allied Arapaho,

Cheyenne, Comanche and Kiowa braves and rode to Adobe Walls to attack the "white-eyes" buffalo hunters. Chiefs Lone Wolf and Woman's Heart and their warriors followed Quanah and set out to fight the buffalo hunters.

Peace Chief Kicking Bird prevented nearly half of the Kiowa warriors from going to war. Chief Quanah led the massive war party, as they swarmed down on Adobe Walls with only twenty three buffalo hunters, who were holed up in the fort. War-cry's cut the silence. The sound was deafening, as the thunder of hoof-beats, rifle cracks and war whoops filled the air.

Seven hundred Indian warriors attacked the fort. About 100 yards from the fort on the first charge, a bullet from a buffalo hunter's long-rifle shot Chief Quanah's horse from under him; the second bullet hit the Chief. The Indians' carbine rifles were no match against the buffalo hunter's sharps rifles. The attack was short-lived and a loss. During the battle, a plainsman's long-rifle bullet struck Ishatai's horse right between the eyes, killing it. His magic yellow paint did not protect his horse from the sniper's bullet. He claimed that his medicine had gone since the warriors had killed a skunk, which he forewarned was taboo. Ishatai lost all credence with his band and spoke with a forked tongue, losing faith in his magic.

With nine Indians slain and only four buffalo hunters dead, the warriors retreated. A seven hundred warrior army could have easily wiped out the white-men with a frontal attack, but the Indians did not like the close quarters.

The fight was named "The Second Battle of Adobe Walls." Some believed it should have been named "The Buffalo Wars," since the Comanche fought over the government law that was passed in order to exterminate all the buffalo in order to defeat the Indians.

Great Comanche Chief Quanah Parker rides in the Parade at Lawton, Oklahoma in 1905

Comanche in Parade in Lawton, Oklahoma, in 1905
Photos Courtesy Western History Collections,
University of Oklahoma Libraries

Chief Quanah Parker finally came in to Fort Sill, and after signing the Treaty of Medicine Lodge he surrendered in 1875, leading the last war party of Comanche Indians on the Southern Plains. Chief Quanah Parker and 400 warriors were the last to relent. On June 2, 1875, Quanah and his Antelope band of Comanche Indians entered Fort Sill, driving 1500 head of horses. This was the end for the "Lords of the Plains." Their control of Comancheria and the Southern Plains was over. The Comanche Indians had ruled for 150 years, but it had ended abruptly.

The Comanche and Kiowa Indians provided a wintering area on the Red River for their horses. This way, they were put out to graze there and could eat the grasses and cottonwood bark. During the summer in 1878, when the bison were scarce, the Kiowa Indians resorted to eating their horses. Other tribes on rare occasions also ate horse flesh to stave off starvation.

The Arapaho, Comanche, and Kiowa of the Southern Plains ravaged the land for hundreds of years. It took the Texas Rangers, and the U.S. Army Cavalry to subdue them. One of the fiercest Indian tribes in America built a mighty nation and was almost unbeatable. Legendary horsemen and brave combatents, they dominated the Plains from the Platte River to Mexico.

The Comanche were a strong foe. Their Indian army had fought the Texas Rangers, the U.S. Army and many Indian contenders. The Comanche Quahadi band faced civilized life among the white man on the reservation, farmed and raised cattle.

Quanah was a peaceable chief treated with respect by the Army. He had fought bravely to save his people. Quanah transitioned to civilized life a wealthy rancher on the reservation, but never forgot his people. He pushed for their education and was appointed Judge of Indian Affairs in 1886. White men tried to get them to divide their reservation and sell to them. Quanah Parker traveled to Washington D.C. in order to change that policy.

CHAPTER SIX
INDIAN PONIES

The Boise Shoshoni were one of the first Shoshoni bands to acquire horses. Their horses grazed on the green grasses of the Boise River bottoms, with good drinking water. The horse was almost as important to the Indians as the invention of fire. We know that the Shoshoni obtained horses over 300 years ago, when the Comanche drove horses up to Fort Hall and to the Boise River Shoshoni and traded stock to their kin. Comanche attended the trade fair hosted by the Boise and Weiser River Shoshoni. The Shoshoni-hosted trade fair was held on a large island on the Snake River, at the confluence of the Boise, Malheur, Owyhee, Payette and Weiser Rivers with the Snake River near present day Payette.

Horses brought change. The "Horse and Indian Era" allowed the Indians freedom of movement during war, food cycles and buffalo hunts. Sheep-eater Shoshoni had few horses. Salmon-eaters were horse-mounted. Weiser Shoshoni became horse people. The Bruneau Snakes (Shoshoni) were walking fish-eater Indians until they joined the Boise Shoshoni band and got horses.

Arapaho, Bannock, Flathead, and Nez Perce Indians met at the Shoshoni Trade center to gamble and trade for horses. Peaceable Indians were welcomed from far and near in the celebrating, dancing, gambling, and trading of arrow heads, arrows, bows, horses, knives, lodge-poles, obsidian, pelts, and other goods. Buffalo hides, robes and other articles were traded for horses. The Northern Mandan and Cheyenne Indians also raised and traded horses at their horse trade centers. Among the Indian tribes that were the most capable horse breeders were the Comanche, Nez Perce and Shoshoni Indians. The Shoshoni Horsemen believed that if a warrior died, all of his horses should be buried with him for the afterlife.

Cheyenne Warrior Rides a Pinto Horse
Photo Courtesy of Azusa Publishing, LLC

The Nez Perce most likely acquired their first ponies and Appaloosas from the Shoshoni Indians that they traded from the Comanche Indians. The Nez Perce developed their favorite breed, the Appaloosa horse, as did their Palouse allies. Appaloosa is the namesake of the Palouse tribe.

The Comanche Horse Indians supplied the Indian tribes of the Northwest and the Central Plains with horses. Another tribe that excelled in breeding horses was the Cayuse Indians, who bred the Cayuse pony, a small buffalo runner. The term "ole Cayuse" referred to a Cayuse pony.

Chief Joseph exhibited his horsemanship during the Nez Perce War handling some 2,000 ponies, while his 300 warriors fought the U.S. Cavalry in a running battle, accompanied by his whole village of men women, and children. In addition, the Nez Perce braves rode on horseback through rugged terrain for 500 plus miles in retreat from the U.S. Army from White Bird Canyon in Idaho to the Bears Paw Mountains where they surrendered.

Pawnee territory paralleled Comanche territory and the Comanche traded horses to them, who traded to them, who in turn traded to the Osage to the east and the Lakota Sioux to the North. The Pawnee prized their horses. A white man visited a Pawnee camp and observed that nearly every family had two or three horses. Some braves had ten ponies; one chief had 30 horses.

In 1805, Lewis and Clark needed canoes and horses for their travel, obtaining horses from the Mandan in trade and from the Cheyenne, Nez Perce and Shoshoni Indians. In the Fur Trade Era, Jim Bridger, Jim Coulter, and "Liver-Eating Johnson" moved into the Rockies to trap for furs. They married Indian wives and trapped beaver; squaws scraped the hides. The mountain men used horses and mules as pack-animals. The Sioux Indians even prayed to their horses as deities. General Crook considered the Sioux

Nez Perce Chief Joseph on Painted Pony
Courtesy of Wikipedia.org

Indian warriors to be the best natural Cavalry of all the Indian tribes and superior in games.

Crazy Horse and Sitting Bull were born the same year. Crazy Horse was born on Rapid Creek in 1831. The parents of Crazy Horse were members of the Oglala band of the Dakota Sioux tribe. They were Plains Indians, dependent on the buffalo.

Sioux tradition tells us the day Crazy Horse was born, a wild horse raced through his village, an omen of greatness in his impending name. As a youth he was called "Curly." As he came of age, he went into the wild to earn his vision quest and had a vision. He envisioned a horse, whose hooves did not touch the ground. It floated, galloped and changed colors as did the attire of Crazy Horse. He rode freely, seeing grass, sky and trees and knew from his vision, he was "Crazy Horse." Fighting the Grass Lodge People, he courageously earned his name, "Crazy Horse."

Crazy Horse had a dream when he was 20 years old and saw himself with trailing, unbraided hair, the feather of a red hawk, and a smooth stone behind his ear. From then on, Crazy horse fought with a river pebble behind his left ear in a leather thong; he sprinkled dust over himself and his horse for power (from legend). Crazy Horse was made one of four "shirt wearers," of the Oglala band, a great honor. Crazy Horse was a medicine man and a mystic who interpreted dreams, but was misunderstood, his life surrounded by mystery. He was a holy man, a shaman, a loner among the Sioux; he never let a photographer take his picture; he believed that the camera would capture his soul. No artist ever sketched a drawing of him or painted Crazy Horse. Crazy Horse loved his childhood sweetheart, the beautiful Black Buffalo Woman, but the union was spoiled by an arranged marriage agreement between her parents and the parents of No Water, a member of Red Cloud's band.

Appaloosa colt- The Nez Perce bred them into fine Breeds. Courtesy of Jumper Horse/Sport

Appaloosa Horse
Photo Courtesy of Azusa
Publishing, LLC

Crazy Horse came back from the war trail to learn she had married No Water, who refused to divorce her. Crazy Horse claimed his bride regardless; No Water threatened to cut off her nose. Briefly, he was with his beloved Black Buffalo Woman once more. They deeply loved each other. Then, No Water burst into their teepee, waved a pistol in the air and fired, tearing under Crazy Horse's cheek, disgracing him. His shirt wearer rank was stripped away. She had no recourse, but to return to No Water.

Crazy Horse rebounded by devoting his time to his role as war chief. The wild warrior Crazy Horse was very brave and daring. He was a tactical genius on the battlefield and a natural born leader and chief. Crazy Horse believed one did not sell Sioux land and is remembered as one of the greatest Sioux Indian chiefs.

Legend tells that Blackfeet war parties rode south for hundreds of miles to New Mexico Territory for horses and stole hundreds of Spanish horses. They were gone over a two-year period, before arriving in Blackfeet Country, trailing stolen horses. They had built up good sized herds of horses. They picked these sturdy ponies as their buffalo horses and probably had the Spanish Mustang, a medium-sized pony, measuring 14 hand spans at the front shoulder weighed around 1,000 pounds.

Horses were trained carefully for months to be buffalo and war horses before riding them into battle or to be used on the hunt to perform correctly when the rider needed both hands on his bow and arrow. In battle it was similar, when hands were free to handle weapons the horse had to remain calm. Plains Indians moved in four seasonal rounds on camp moves from one food source to the next. The horse mounted Plains Indians traveled on horseback to hunt, in battle, and to trail pack animals, f o r transportation, in seasonal rounds, and for racing their horses. A number of ponies made bride-price. Indians loved their horses.

Iconic Photo of Sioux Chief
Photo Courtesy of Azusa Publishing, LLC

The Old North Trail ran south from present day Calgary on the eastern slope of the Rocky Mountains, south, not encompassing the hills or mountains, to where Helena now stands, southward reaching into Mexico. Blackfeet Indians have a tradition that their horses came from the Shoshoni Indian people.

According to legend, the first time the Blackfeet saw a horse, was when the Shoshoni attacked them on horses in 1730. Piegan Blackfeet attained horses shortly after the Shoshoni and distributed them to the Blood and Siksika bands in Montana and to the Blackfoot horse culture in Canada. Assiniboine Indians garnered firearms early from the Hudson's Bay Company. The Assiniboine, Blackfeet and Cree formed an alliance against the Shoshoni and attacked a large Shoshoni war party. Blackfeet, living in Montana, were semi-nomadic and constantly raided the Shoshoni, Bannock, Flathead, Nez Perce villages and other tribes for horses in the area now known as Idaho.

Horses were painted red on one side and blue on the other for the Horse Dance. The Blackfeet favored red paint on their horses. Bridles, saddles and pommels were heavily beaded. Their ponies were adorned with ribbons tied to the manes and tails. Warriors on horses circled and charged in mock battle, gave war whoops, and shrill war cries, while firing rifles in the air. Legend tells us that Blackfeet war parties rode south for hundreds of miles, reaching the Spanish colonies in New Mexico for horses. They stole hundreds of Spanish Cayuses.

The Blackfeet Indians journeyed to New Mexico and returned with a large string of horses, including Spanish Mustangs. An old Piegan chief, Brings-Down–the-Sun, described Piegan war parties returning on the trail in 1787, with horses stolen in Mexico.

Sioux Women Traveling on Horseback
Photo Courtesy of Azusa Publishing, LLC

Blackfeet Indian Buffalo Runner
Photo Courtesy
www.aaanativearts.com

They prized the Spanish Mustang as a buffalo runner and war horse. Mustang in Blackfeet was "wakiya." Spanish Mustang was one of the finest horses in America, circa 1600.

The Blackfeet captured a magnificent black stallion, which broke loose and became a killer. It stole mares to build his herd and caused great destruction of property. The Ghost Horse was like a phantom running in the night; its blue black coat was unseen in the darkness; its mane and tail shining in the moonlight.

Spotted horses were sacred to the Indians, who thought they had magical powers. Plains Indians regarded the Medicine Hat Horse as sacred from legend. The Indians painted symbols on them. They were used as a Ceremonial Horses, Buffalo Runners, and War Horses believed to have a magical ability to protect its rider from death or injury in battle and warn their riders of danger. They were special medicine, considered supernatural and believed that they offered protection from harm from the Sioux Indians.

Some War Bonnet horses were valued by Native Americans, because they had a color on the chest called a shield to protect them and their rider in battle. Only chiefs, medicine men and warriors were allowed to ride them.

The Medicine Hat (War Bonnet Horse) is a beautiful white pinto horse with rare pattern of color having dark blotches around the ears and on top of the head resembling a bonnet or hat. They often have pink muzzles. Those with one or both blue eyes are especially prized; some have dark eyes surrounded by white. War Bonnet is a name given to horses of a similar pattern. They may be of any base color. Medicine Hats are described by their base color such as bay Medicine Hat, black roan Medicine Hat, and chestnut Medicine Hat etc.

For thousands of years, domestic dogs were utilized by the Ute Indians to carry loads. Small packs were strapped on the dogs'

Plainswoman, Horse & Travois
Courtesy Azusa Publishing
Company, LLC

backs to carry supplies. Another method used was the travois pulled by dogs. The horse brought change to the Indian life by replacing the dog pulling the travois, a simple vehicle used by the Plains Indians consisting of two crossed trailing poles joined by a frame bearing a load, drug behind a horse. The horse drawn travois transported goods and infants. The poles were also used for tipis.

The Pawnee Indians in Nebraska lodged next to Comanche country and were privy to the horse though trade and by theft. It was said that a Pawnee chief might have owned as many as 30 horses. A warrior had 8-12 and even a poor family had 2-3 horses.

The Kiowa Indians most likely got their first horses from the Crow Indians in 1748, when they dwelled in the Rocky Mountain country in the north. The Crow originally got horses from the Comanche. A Comanche chief rebuked the Kiowa for not traveling to Mexico to take them. He said that the last time that he saw them they only had dogs and sleds.

A Coeur d'Alene Indian legend told the story of how a Kalispell Indian rode into their village one day. These Indians had never seen a horse before. The people became excited wondering about the strange animal. The beast seemed gentle and they examined it thoroughly. They could ride it and many did, but when it trotted they fell off. Then the Kalispell rode away.

Indians controlled the Plains for nearly 200 years with the horse. The "Era of the Horse and Buffalo" was good for the Indians. Romance between the horse and Indian was short lived. Horses changed the American Indians' culture in its entirety and transformed the Indians' life way.

The U.S. Army first shot and killed the Indian's horses by the thousands to limit their movement and transitioned the Indians onto reservations beginning in 1867, confiscated their guns and the Indian Wars were over. The Indians had fought long and hard for their homeland and lost. War, disease and starvation had won out.

CHAPTER SEVEN
CIVIL WAR HORSES

The War between the North and South began over major differences. The North was chiefly industrial, while the South was agrarian. Cotton was their major crop and source of wealth. It took African slaves to pick the cotton. A slave could be bought, sold or traded, like an animal. A steady flow of immigrants came to America during the Irish famine of 1840-1850 with plenty of laborers in the work force with no slaves. After 1840, during the industrial period the horse and mule population grew twice as fast as the human population. In 1855, a new political party arose as the Whig party died out. The Republican party opposed slavery. Pastors, churches, and Abolitionists opposed slavery.

In 1857, the Dred Scott Decision disallowed slaves from becoming citizens. John Brown raided Harper's Ferry as an attempt to arm the Negroes in 1859. The Fugitive Slave Act was passed. President Buchanan refused to arbitrate between the North and the South. Northern newspapers campaigned against states rights.

The northerners did not like slavery and the Northern states abolished slavery one state at a time. On the eve of the Civil War, 4 million African slaves toiled in the South. Slaves were essential to pick cotton. The South decided to establish a new confederation of states. In 1860, Abraham Lincoln won the election for the presidency. After the election, most of the southern states seceded from the Union. The question of slavery caused rebellion and ushered in the Civil War. The Battle of Fort Sumter was fought near Charleston, South Carolina on April 12-14, 1861. The bombardment and surrender of Fort Sumter started the Civil War after the declaration of secession of seven slave states in the South. South Carolina demanded that the U.S. Army vacate and abandon its facilities in Charleston Harbor.

Battle of Fort Sumter
Photo Courtesy of Wikipedia.org

President Lincoln immediately called up 75,000 volunteers to put down the rebellion. Four more Southern slave states seceded and joined the Confederacy. The Civil War had begun. At the start of the war, the Union Cavalry was superior.

The "Rebels" were credited with being plow boys used to being raised around horses and were used to stables and race tracks. Southern race horses were the American Saddle-bred and the Tennessee Walking stock of superior breeds. These horses could be ridden in comfort. They were known for endurance and a smooth gait. Morgan horses were small and sturdy, a quality horse and were used by the North and South. A few Arabians were used.

Horses were of major importance during the Civil War in America. Horses and mules pulled Army ambulances that carried guns and ammunition. Horses pulled supply trains and carried messages, troops, and generals. They were strong and courageous. The movement of the Civil War depended on horses.

Congress authorized six Regular U.S. Cavalry regiments; the states contributed 272 Cavalry regiments to federal service. In 1861, the North and South both utilized horse-mounted Cavalry in the Civil War. The war was hard on horses. They were shot, overworked, broke their legs, and contracted diseases and died.

In the Cavalry during the Civil War, General George Armstrong Custer had many narrow escapes and had eleven horses shot from under him, only receiving one wound from a Confederate artillery shell and was known for his "Custer luck."

Horses were needed in battle for the Cavalry. Horses persevered in choking heat and dust. They plodded along quietly and could run at a gallop into the midst of battle. Some horses were wounded. They were shot and injured like their masters and died bravely. The horses fought bravely like their masters in battle. In the beginning more horses and mules were killed than soldiers.

Horses were taught on command how to act during battle conditions and react under fire. One tactic was for the horses to lie down on command under cross-fire from machine guns to avoid injury. One final test before the horses went into battle was to endure live machine gun fire passing over their heads. The rider dismounted and the horse was told to lie down. If the animal minded and lay unharmed, it passed the test. Horses went through the same danger as soldiers and fought to stay alive.

Horses and mules killed at Gettysburg alone totaled over 1500. The Confederacy lost 619 horses and mules; the Union lost 881. Horses suffering from fatigue had to be put down. Hundreds of horses died from exhaustion and disease. One trick in battle was to shoot the horses attached to a battery, disabling the unit. Horses and mules killed during the Civil War totaled one million.

Ration for an artillery horse was 14 pounds of hay and 12 pounds of barley, corn and oats contingent on the size of the battery. The daily portion was huge. An artillery battery might sit immobile for weeks at a time and yet consume tons of hay and grain. Pasture fodder was sometimes fed, but field plants and grasses were not efficient. Eighty pounds of greens were needed to equal 26 pounds of dry grain and hay as daily nutrition. A steady diet of greens might cause horses to founder and become lame, but pasturage could be used as a supplement for a short period of time. Another must for the horses was an adequate water supply. An envoy had to leave camp to locate the nearest creek, lake or pond in order to provide enough drinking water for the horses.

Artillery horses represented a smaller number of animals that had to be fed by the military. Thousands of horses and mules served the artillery by pulling wagons and as saddle horses for curriers and officers. Feed for a brigade of horses totaled 800,000 pounds of grain and forage per day. With a tremendous need for hay and grain for the horses, it created a huge demand on both sides. Lack of feed and water created a serious shortage on both sides. Usually, a shortage of wagons was the problem. After the wagons made deliveries, the infantry seized them for ambulances.

The feat for a healthy work horse was to pull an average load of 3,000 pounds 20 miles a day over a hard paved road. The weight pulled dropped to 1900 pounds on a paved road and 1100 pounds over a rough road. The pulling capacity of one horse was reduced to 700 pounds in a team. Mules were commonly used to pull artillery. Horses were substituted when guns went into action. In the Civil War a band of Cavalry with a battery of mountain howitzers loaded on mules came under fire. The men took cover in a ravine that offered some shelter. Mules in fear kicked, lunged, squealed, and tried to shake off their loads. Each mule carried 300 pounds. It took three men to hold down one mule.

Once, during the Battle of Chattanooga, mules actually helped win a battle. Under heavy fire, teamsters became scared and fled; the mules broke and ran straight toward enemy lines. The Confederates thought it was a Cavalry charge and deserted.

The Northern states possessed 3.4 million horses at the start of the Civil War. The Southern states had 1.7 million. There were hundreds of thousands of horses in reserve on both sides and 100,000 mules in the North. One horse cost $150. Most of the fighting was done on Southern soil. It was easy for the Bluecoats to take horses and mules from the Confederacy not to gain more horses, but to deprive the Confederates of horses. Southern troops did not capture nearly as many. The Confederates stole 100's of horses, compared to the Union Army's 1,000's.

General Ulysses S. Grant led the Union Army to victory, defeating Robert E. Lee in 1865. It was a bitter war with many casualties. Congress worked toward reconstruction and to free the South of slavery. That year, President Abraham Lincoln was assassinated.

The Stagecoach of the "Old West"
Photo Courtesy of Wikipedia.org

CHAPTER EIGHT
HORSES OF THE OLD WEST

During the Fur Trade Era, mountain men migrated southward from Canada into te Rocky Mountains to trap for furs in 1811. Famous trappers like Jim Bridger, Jim Coulter, and "Liver Eating Johnson" were noted fur traders. Fur trappers took Indian squaws as wives and lived like the Indians. To travel and haul their goods, the mountain men used horses and mules. They trapped beaver; their Indian wives scraped the hides.

Horses were the mode of transportation in the West. The horse is synonymous with the West. Settlers began to come west in 1842. Horses, mules, and oxen pulled covered wagons westward along the Oregon Trail to Oregon. Oxen had great strength to pull the Conestoga wagons, but became overheated easily. Mules had great stamina and could travel 20 miles a day. Horses were used to pull covered wagons because they were more readily available. Horses pulled buckboards, buggies and pulled plows so that they could plant crops. Ponies were saddled and ridden for everyday transportation, work and pleasure.

Settlers in the West established ranches with corrals and barns to hold horses and strung barb-wire fences to pen cattle. Cowboys rode out to capture wild horses and caught and broke the wild Cayuses. Feral horses were caught and roped with lariats and were sold in Mexico.

Horses were first used in the state militia prior to 1832. In June of 1832, Congress approved a Battalion of Mounted Rangers. They were a success and in 1833, Congress approved an even larger unit and called it the Regiment of Dragoons after Europe had success with them. Additional regiments of mounted troops were formed called the Regiment of Mounted Riflemen, armed with the model 1841 rifle over the common musket of the times.

In 1846, the United States went to war with Mexico, which was fought primarily on horseback and with foot soldiers. The Mexican Cavalry rode Spanish Colonial horses.

The U.S. Army Cavalry began in 1855. The U.S. Army Cavalry and the Texas Rangers were outfitted with horses. These were horse-mounted Cavalry fighting units equipped with Colt Navy pattern pistols. When the Indian Wars broke out in 1855, President Lincoln assigned Cavalry out West to fight the Indians.

In 1858, the first Overland Mail Stage Coach completed its run from St. Louis to San Francisco that was 2800 miles with stops at numerous stations having plenty of grass and water for the horses. The Pony Express service officially opened April 3, 1860, when riders left simultaneously from St. Joseph, Missouri and Sacramento, California. The Pony Express was founded in Sacramento by Alexander Majors, William H. Russell and William Waddell. A speedy mail service was spurred on by the threat of Civil War. The Pony Express consisted of relays of young riders carrying mailbags on horseback across a 2,000 mile stretch with 400-500 horses, yet only one mailbag was lost. The service just lasted for 19 months, when the Pacific Telegraph line took its place. The Pony Express had 100 stations, and 80 riders.

Comanche was a Mustang purchased by the U.S. Army Cavalry in 1868. He got his name after being shot during battle by an Indian arrow. The wounded horse screamed in agony, which prompted a soldier to comment that he shrieked like a Comanche Indian; thus his name. On the morning of June 25th, 1876, General Custer led his soldiers of the 7th Cavalry against the Sioux Indians at the Little Bighorn. As the battle ended all 273 men of the 7th Cavalry were killed as were 80 Indians. The only survivor was Captain Keogh's horse, Comanche, from Custer's detachment. The Indians had previously caught the rest of the ponies.

Comanche survived the Little Bighorn
Photo Courtesy of Wikipedia.org

Comanche was found two days later badly wounded and was taken to Fort Lincoln, North Dakota to recuperate, and made a full recovery. Comanche never fought again, but became a celebrity during his retirement and took part in many celebrations and parades. Comanche was a symbol of Custer, the 7th Cavalry, and their memory. Today, Comanche is stuffed and stands on display at the Kansas University Museum of Natural History.

The Old "Chism Trail" was a cattle trail used from 1867 to 1884, a major route out of Texas for livestock. Longhorn cattle were driven north along the trail. Cattle sales became a steady source of income for the impoverished state of Texas recovering from the Civil War. Demand for beef in the East in 1881 created a need for cattle. Jesse Chism brought trade goods in 1864 to Indian villages near modern day Wichita about 220 miles south of his post. The name, Chism Trail was given to the route from central Kansas to the Rio Grande. Cowhands rode spirited Mustangs to drive thousands of head of cattle over the old Chism Trail, the term used by major newspapers referring to the famous route.

The Army planned to block the supply route between the Powder River Country in Wyoming and the Red Cloud and the Spotted Tail Agencies in Nebraska. On July 17, 1876, the Fifth U.S. Army planned to block the supply route between the Powder River Country in Wyoming and the Red Cloud and the Spotted Tail Agencies in Nebraska.

On July 17, 1876, the Fifth U.S. Army Cavalry, under Colonel Wesley Merit engaged the Cheyenne Indians in battle near the Red Cloud Agency on northwestern Nebraska and southeastern Wyoming. One of the scouts in the fight was William F. Cody, known as "Buffalo Bill." Will also worked as a scout for George Armstrong Custer, fought the Sioux Indians and admired them for their courage. On patrol, he led a company into battle against the hostile Cheyenne.

During the battle, Cody shot the horse out from beneath a Cheyenne war chief, named Yellow Hand in a duel; his second shot

102

"Buffalo Bill" Cody & Chief Sitting Bull
Courtesy of Azusa Publishing, L.L.C.

killed him. He held up his scalp and war bonnet and claimed the prize for Custer. Cody bragged after the fight. The account of Cody's fight appeared in the New York Herald.

Buffalo Bill Cody went on the road with his stage play, "Scouts of the Prairie," a drama created by dime-novelist, Ned Buntline, who developed Buffalo Bill's character into *Prince of the Plains* for his biography. He played in Chicago with Texas Jack and Wild Bill Hickok. Cody played himself in Buntline's stage play called "Buffalo Bill" in New York. By 1875, he had written several books: *Deadly Eye, Prairie Prince, The Boy Outlaw, Scout* and *The Renegade*.

In 1882, the people of North Platte asked Cody to hold a rodeo. Cody's Wild West Show had included historical events, races, and sharpshooting. Buffalo Bill Cody co-owned a ranch near North Platte, Nebraska, the Scouts Rest Ranch, where he resided. Cody boasted of his feats, was a heavy drinker and a braggart.

Never-the-less, he built a western show across the nation, and was well loved. Gordon W. Lillie, later known as Pawnee Bill, was an interpreter at the Fort Sill Indian reservation. Bill borrowed Sioux Indians for his 1877-78 stage show, written by A.S. Burt, based on the Mountain Meadows Massacre, and involved Mormons and Indians ambushing a wagon train. Will's show included "Scouts of the Plains," which included Buffalo Bill, Texas Jack, and "Wild Bill Hickok." They acted out skits about the Plains.

The Sioux tribe was a popular Plains tribe and became the model for the characterization of the American Indian. A Sioux appeared on the Indian head penny and the buffalo nickel. So Will Cody used wild Sioux Indians in his performances of the Wild West Show and made the Sioux famous.

"Buffalo Bill" Cody
Courtesy of Azusa Publishing, L.L.C.

Buffalo Bill's Wild West Show, North Platte, Nebraska,
Courtesy of Azusa Publishing, L.L.C.

In June of 1885, Buffalo Bill sent Major Burke to the reserve at the Standing Rock Agency to speak with Sitting Bull, medicine man of the Sioux. He wanted Chief Sitting Bull to appear in his Wild West Show in the Indian Village. Sitting Bull left the reservation in 1885 to join the Wild West. Major Burke employed the chief and other Indians. Sitting Bull made a number of public appearances and visited Bismarck, North Dakota to meet with General Grant and headed a parade celebrating the opening of the Northern Pacific Railroad Transcontinental line. Buffalo Bill made friends with Sitting Bull, who was devoted to Will. Sitting Bull called him "*Pahaska*," (in the Sioux tongue Long Hair).

Sioux Indians that appeared in Buffalo Bill's Wild West Show were American Horse, Amos-Little-Sioux, Amos-Two-Bulls, Arthur-Standing Bear, Bad Bear, Bear Tales, Black Elk, Flying Hawk, Has-No-Horses, High Heron, Indian-With-Rifle, In–the-West–Was–Destroying, Iron Shell, Iron Tail, Iron-White-Man, Joe-Black-Fox, Kicking-Bear-Bonnet, Kills-Close-to-the-Lodge, Long Bull, Long Wolf, Red Cloud, Red Shirt, Sammy-Lone Bear, Sioux-Indian-Man-Named-Kills, and Sitting Bull. Indians rode on horseback giving war whoops and terrifying the crowd.

Women sometimes out-rode and out-gunned the men with a six-gun. Annie Oakley was certainly one of those. She was an expert marksman and the most famous woman of her time. Chief Sitting Bull called her "Little Sure Shot," with endearment.

Will featured various animals in his show like buffalo, cattle, elk, horses and other mammals. Buffalo Bill used a troop of real cowboys and cowgirls that he recruited from ranches out West. Many people referred to cowboys as coarse cattle drivers, using the term cowboys as an insult, but by the end of the 19th century cowboys were mentioned with much love. Buffalo Bill's Wild West Show was the very first Rodeo in America and the forerunner of the modern rodeo of today.

CHAPTER NINE
HORSEPOWER

The horse made its mark in the East as well as out West. There was a time when America derived its power from the horse. This power could thresh wheat or saw logs. Yes, it was the horse that gained new admiration, but the steam engine eventually replaced the horse. This worked well as harnessed horsepower, but in late 1872, the horse flu spread across America sickening seven out of eight horses. Horse-pulled freight could not be delivered. Horse-drawn streetcars could not run. Wharves and railroad depots were shut down. Consumers lacked ice, groceries and milk without ponies. Brickyards, construction sites and factories were helpless with no horses. Fire protection and garbage collection were crippled. Saloons ran out of beer. Horses actually pulled locomotives. Animal power was the only option in the 19th century. Oxen pulled the farm plows, replaced by draft horses.

Draft-horse is a term used to describe carthorses, heavy horses or workhorses. During the 1800's, draft-horses were employed for multiple tasks in America utilized in farming, logging, and sports horses. Lighter breeds were saddled. They varied in size from a muscular draft-horse to lighter riding horses.

Ponies have been in the Shetland Isles for 2,000 years dating back to the Bronze Age. People believe that they were domesticated. It is believed the early horse was a Mountain pony from Southern Europe that migrated over ice fields and land masses. The pony was later introduced to the Celts, who crossed it with the Oriental horse. Two significant types evolved within the breed: a heavier boned horse with a longer head and a lighter pony with a high tail and pretty head. The characteristics have remained over time. Shetland ponies are hardy horses. Legend tells that Shetlands ate seaweed on the ocean shores during cold winters.

Team Pulling Plow
Photo Courtesy of Wikipedia.org

In 1847, the pony was used to work in the mines. The small horses have a gentle nature, worked well with their owners, and were loved by their handlers. Excellent studs were used to breed the large structured Shetland horses for work in the pits. The strength of the Shetland pony for their size put them above all horse breeds. Ponies cultivated the land for centuries and hauled peat and seaweed to the fields. The pony also transported its owner. Pony owner fishermen also used horse hair for fish line.

Shetland ponies are popular with children to ride. Queen Victoria had owned several Shetland ponies. Thousands of ponies were exported across the Atlantic in the 19th century. Shetland Stud Book Society was established in 1890 in Britain. Many of the pedigreed ponies can be traced to the society. Blood lines are traced that way. Descendents came from pedigreed British studs.

A draft-horse developed in England was the Shire horse that was used specifically for pulling carts from the dock to the industries.

The American Shire Horse Association was established in the 19th century. Shire workhorses were used extensively for farming. Huge Shire horses have an enormous capacity for pulling loads. Shire stallions are usually bay, black or grey and do not have white markings. Mares can be bay, black, grey, or roan. Stallions stand 17.2 hands high (70 inches) and mares stand at least 16 hands high (64 inches) and weigh 2,000-2,400 pounds. The Shire head is long and lean, with large eyes and a long slightly arched neck. The shoulder and chest are wide. The back is short and muscular. The hindquarter is long and wide. Shire horses made good workhorses.

Horses replaced oxen in pulling plows made from cast iron and steel. McCormick threshing machines and bailing machines were pulled by horses. Horses urbanized 40% faster than humans. By 1890, thousands of railroad horses were in New York City.

Shetland Pony
Photo Courtesy of Wikipedia.org

CHAPTER TEN
RODEOS

Rodeos began in Spain and Mexico. Rodeos were adopted in America in 1882 with the first western rodeo on the Fourth of July at North Platte, Nebraska and continue today. Buffalo Bill Cody held America's first rodeo called "the Old Glory Blowout," and performed his Wild West Show. The next year he held his rodeo in Columbus, Nebraska. Cody loved kids and gave tickets to orphanages. His show was based on the "Old West."

The word, rodeo came from a Spanish word, which translated "round up." Rodear in Spanish meant to encompass and refers to a pen for cattle used at a fair or market. Rodeo is further translated or derived from rotar in Latin meaning to go around.

In Spain, a rodeo was a time for vaqueros to move cattle to new pastures, or to sell or slaughter mavericks. The word rodeo in Spain referred to the skills of ranch hands, which translated in the American rodeo. In 1834, the word was used in America for the round up of cattle. Today, the word rodeo describes an exhibition of cowboys performing for the public in an arena. Rodeos followed in Australia, Canada and New Zealand. The rodeo is a competitive sport that arose from cattle herding in Spain. The sport began with the working skills of the Spanish Vaquero.

The events run from spring until December. The rodeo is one of the most popular sporting events in the U.S.A. There are 25 top rodeos in America. Talented cowboys compete for big purses as prize money. Rodeos have been a top sport for 120 years. Rodeos are popular across America.

Rodeos today involve cattle, horses, and some sheep. Professional rodeos in America involve testing the skill of both cowboys and cowgirls in contests, barrel racing, bareback bronco riding, bull riding, saddle bronco riding, steer wrestling team roping,

Rodeo Bull Riding
Photo Courtesy of Wikipedia.org

Wyoming Rodeo
Photo Courtesy of Wikipedia.org

and tie-down roping. The events are divided into two categories: rough stock events and timed events. Kid's events, such as sheep riding is a specialty.

Stock contractors that own rodeo livestock provide animals for rodeo events. The professional rodeo horses are bred to have the inclination to buck. The rodeo horses are kept in the spirit because they continue to buck their riders off. The bucking horse is considered too dangerous to be in other venues, yet they fit in well with the bareback bronco riding and the saddle bronco riding competition in the rodeo.

There are two types of bucking horses: horses used in the saddle bronco contest and horses used in the bareback riding event. Bareback horses are smaller ponies that buck harder. Saddleback horses on the whole are larger and have a classic way of bucking allowing the rider to sit up in the saddle to the rhythm of the motion to spur the pony. Saddle bronco horses are often a draft horse-mix. These big sturdy horses have the qualities of a classic bucking horse that retain the strength and endurance to complete the task for a cowboy's ride over time in the horses' rodeo life.

Horses are supposed to buck and meet the challenge. Surprisingly, if horses buck too much, they are sold. One such horse that was sold could not be trained. A famous California trainer took the horse and entered it in the bucking horse competition and found the horse to be a winner. The gelding bucked in the PRCA for 17 years and was named Bareback Bucking Horse of the Year in 1981. When he turned 24, the champion was semi retired to the Pro Rodeo Hall of Fame in Colorado Springs. Classic Velvet ran another three years and finally was put out to pasture in Guffey, Colorado with other stock.

Rodeos are a favorite event in America. They usually are held during mid to late summer. There is a Professional Rodeo Cowboys Association (PRCA) and a Women's Professional

Calf Roping at a Modern Rodeo
Photo Courtesy of Wikipedia.org

Bronco Rider
Photo Courtesy of Wikipedia.org

Association the (WPRA). Other associations govern children's, collegiate, high school, and senior rodeos in America.

Some organizations for animal rights oppose rodeos like the SPCA. The American rodeo industry has made changes and improved the treatment of rodeo animals, but it remains under the scrutiny of rodeos in America and Canada. Some rodeos have been banned there and around the world.

One popular rodeo race in America is the Wild Horse Race. Wild horses behind a chute cross the line. Then, they can be saddle. Cruelty to the ponies is barred. All of the loose horses are available to mount. When the horse is saddled and the rider mounted, the lead rope is removed. The first contestant and his horse to cross the white line is the winner. Ties are judged by a coin toss. Three-way ties are paid per event. The high dollar team in all four shows won buckles.

Rodeos across America are like mom and apple pie. The rodeo has been a tradition for over 100 years. Rodeos have become a national sport enjoyed by thousands of Americans. Many hundreds of cowboys have paid their entry fees and competed. Cowboys and cowgirls alike compete. Thousands of cows and horses are used in rodeos.

Cheyenne Frontier Days is the world's largest outdoor rodeo and Western festival. Houston, Texas boasts the world's largest indoor rodeo. Fort Worth and Houston have rodeos that attract millions of fans every year.

Reno and Las Vegas have good rodeos with bucking bronco riding, bucking bulls, saddle and bareback riding, barrel racing and rodeo clowns. Cowboys compete, as do the cowgirls in events. There is mutton busting for the kids.

Denver features a Mexican extravaganza and includes a bull fight. 1,000 cowboys attend yearly to compete. The largest beef breeder show in the U.S. occurs at the time of the rodeo.

American Horse Racing
Photo Courtesy of Wikipedia.org

Harness Racing
Photo Courtesy of Wikipedia.org

CHAPTER ELEVEN
HORSE RACING

The first Kentucky Derby was run on May 17, 1875 and consisted of well groomed Thoroughbred horses that were a cross between Arabian stallions and European mares, 15 excellent jockeys, the majority of whom were African American. The chestnut colt named Aristides ran the Kentucky Derby in Louisville at the 1.5 mile stakes race. Oliver Lewis was riding Aristides in that race and crossed the finish line ahead of the pack that day in Louisville, Kentucky as the crowd in the bleachers around the track cheered. Aristides was named after an ancient Greek general won the very first Kentucky Derby Race.

Horse racing is popular in America and dates back to 1665 in New York. Three racing classics began in the 19th century: the Belmont Stakes, Kentucky Derby and Preakness Stakes. On June 19, 1867, the first annual race was won by Ruthless. The Preakness Stakes had its first run on May 27, 1873. A bay named Survivor won that race in 2:43 on a 1.187 mile track.

On June 6, 2015, for the first time in 37 years, American Pharoah won the Triple Crown in front of 90,000 spectators. His jockey was Victor Espinoza and his trainer was Bob Baffert. The three year old bay colt was only the twelfth horse to win the Triple Crown. He passed the eight horse field early. American Pharoah won by 51/2 lengths, followed by Frosted and Keen Ice was third in the one and one half mile racetrack. The horse had previously won the Kentucky Derby and the Preakness before his triumph at Belmont as the Triple Crown winner.

Triple Crown winners: 1919-Sir Barton, 1930-Gallant Fox, 1935-Omaha, 1937-War Admiral, 1941-Whirlaway, 1943-Count Fleet, 1946-Assault, 1948-Citation, 1973-Secretariat, 1977-Seattle Slew, 1978-Affirmed, 2015-American Pharoah.

Another type of racing is Harness Racing, a national sport sulky). Race horses reach speeds of 30 miles per hour. It is a big betting sport worldwide and is a great recreational activity.

In Harness racing the trot or pace is used instead of the gallop. When the race horses run the pace race, legs on the same side of the body move in unison, identified by the straps around all four legs called hobbles. This helps them maintain their gait. Pace races are faster and more popular.

In trotter races, diagonal legs move in unison. Trotting is a more natural gait with no straps, but some do wear loops on the front legs to maintain rhythm. These are called rotting hobbles. Horses are bred to perform their particular gait. Some are able to switch gaits. Most race at the same gait as did their ancestors.

Horse jumping is one of the most popular and perhaps most recognizable equestrian events, aside from Thoroughbred horse racing. Jumping horses began in England and includes English riding equestrian games known as dressage, equitation and hunters. At its highest competitive level, show jumping is recognized as one of the three Olympic equestrian disciplines.

Show jumping is known as open jumping. The horses are referred to as jumpers. Jumping classes are commonly seen at horse shows around the world and the Olympics. Other times jumping is included in a vast spectrum of English style events.

Show jumping has been adopted in America and is a favorite sport in the states. Show jumping is a national sport in America and internationally. There are various national organizations that can sanction horse jumping like the United States Equestrian Federation Sports.

American Pharoah
Photo Courtesy of Wikipedia.org

Jumping Horse
Photo Courtesy of Wikipedia

Beautiful Jim Key
Public Domain

CHAPTER TWELVE
FAMOUS HORSES

The Beautiful Jim Key was a very amazingly smart horse trained by an ex slave, Dr. William Key at the turn of the twentieth century. Jim Key could determine a letter printed on a card and was rewarded by a sugar cube for performing the trick correctly. William's wife asked the horse if it wanted an apple and it nodded. So Williams trained the horse to nod no in order to answer a question. After that William asked Jim Key questions and he nodded to the affirmative. His owner demonstrated that Jim Key could make correct change from a cash register. Jim Key, the wonder horse appeared in hundreds of shows. William believed in treating Jim Key with kindness, never beating him. Jim performed at the 1904 World's Fair and also for President William McKinley.

During the Korean War, a young Korean girl stepped on a land mine and had her leg blown off. To purchase a prosethetic leg, her brother sold the Marine outfit a chestnut Mongolian mare for $250.00. Marines named the mare "Reckless," after their weapons, the "reckless rifles." She served the Marines by carrying anti-tank ammunition to the front lines and was loved and admired by her fellow marines. She was fearless under fire. During the Battle of Outpost Vegas, Reckless carried 9,000 pounds of ammunition to the front lines, having made one round trip a day for 51 days of Outpost Vegas. Being a Marine, reckless enjoyed eating scrambled eggs and drinking an occasional beer. The mare was so loved that the Marines promoted her to the rank of Staff Sergeant. The Saturday Evening Post featured an article on her story. The mare was brought to the United States and retired at Camp Pendleton, California. A bronze statue of Reckless now stands at the National Museum of the Marine Corps in Triangle, Virginia. Reckless is still remembered and loved today.

Staff Sergeant Reckless
Public Domain

Pinto and owner, George Beck
Public Domain

Pinto is the only horse to have walked across the Continental United States, a distance of 20,352 miles. It is the longest documented trek of the 20th century. In 1912 professional horseman George Beck and four other men from Shelton, Washington decided to make history by reaching every state capital in America on horseback. On June 1, 1915, they arrived in San Francisco with not enough interest to promote their story.

Publicity Photo of Roy Rogers & Trigger
Photo Courtesy of roy_rogers_and_trigger.jpg

Roy Rogers is a famous cowboy from the movies and television. His horse, trigger was trained to come when Roy whistled. The palomino did many tricks and even said his prayers. The animal certainly was intelligent and had lots of young fans in movie-land. Roy's wife in real life was Dale Evans, who played on the set. Her horse, by the way, was named Butter-milk. Bullet, their trusty German shepherd, was a highly trained stunt dog that was active in their movies.

Laura Wilson

The famous photographer, Laura Wilson, photographed many Hutterite subjects at a religious colony in Montana. One such feat was the "Hutterite Boy balancing on an Appaloosa horse." In addition, Wilson wrote the book, "Hutterites of Montana." Photo Courtesy of Laura Wilson.

Famous Cowboy Gene Autry & Champion
Photo Courtesy of Wikipedia.org

Gene was born Orvon Gene Autry on September 29, 1907 in Tioga, Texas. His mother died when he was four. He moved to Oklahoma where he sang in the local church. Gene learned the guitar and was recognized for his singing by Will Rogers in 1926.

In 1927, Gene was hired to sing on the radio in Tulsa, as the "Yodeling Oklahoma Cowboy." Autry had his first hit with the song he wrote called, That Silver-Haired Daddy of Mine." Autry's success got him a job on the "National Barn Dance."

Gene went on to make his radio debut in the 1930's. In 1935, Autry made his first movie and starred in "The Phantom Empire," and "Tumbling Tumbleweeds," the same year and was credited as writing the first musical western. Soon Gene was dubbed the "Singing Cowboy." Other films he starred in were "Rhythm of the Saddle" and "Sioux City Sue" in 1938.

Autry was a shrewd business man, who developed and promoted his western themed merchandise during WWII. Gene enlisted in the Army Air Force and served from 1942-1945. In 1949 Gene returned to the musical charts with his all time hit, "Rudolph the Red-Nosed Reindeer."

Gene Autry and his trusty horse, Champion were the rage back then. I know that he was my hero. In 1950, Autry produced and starred in his own television series, "The Gene Autry Show" and retired from acting in the 60's after six successful seasons.

Autry was a film star, guitarist, television actor, and recording artist. Gene acted in his movies from 1930-1960 and was the recipient of two Grammy Hall of Fame Awards for his talent. Autry had five stars on the Hollywood Walk of Fame and owned the Anaheim Angels Major League Baseball team from 1961 to 1997. He lost his wife in 1980 remarried and established the Autry National Center of the American West museum. Gene died on October 2, 1998, in Studio City, California at the ripe old age of 91 years old.

Clint Eastwood in Movie
Photo Courtesy of Wikipedia.org

After some lesser parts in B films in Hollywood, like "Revenge of the Creature and Tarantula," Clint Eastwood got his first big role in the popular series, "Rawhide." He made it into America's hearts in the roll of the handsome Rowdy Yates in the TV series.

It was not long before he appeared on the big screen and became an icon on the international cinema set. America loved the spagghetti westerns like "The Good, The Bad and the Ugly," "A Fist Full of Dollars," "For a Few Dollars More," "Hang 'Em High," "Two Mules for Sister Sarah," "Joe Kidd," "Pale Rider," "High Plains Drifter," "The Outlaw Josey Wales," "Bronco Billy," "Any Way You Can," and "Paint Your Wagon," with Lee Marvin. The name of Clint's horse in Pale Rider was "Coaly."

Clint Eastwood has earned an oscar for Best Actor and Best Director. Clint fits right in to the brawling, fast draw, at home and with a rifle. Best known for his cowboy roles, Eastwood fills the character of the handsome, rough, tough man on his spirited horse with a six-gun, who's not afraid of trouble.

The Tim Holts, Gene Autrys, Rex Allens, John Waynes, and Roy Rogers of the past give way to the romancing, gun-toting, horsemounted role of the western hero filled by the much loved actor, Clint Eastwood. When Clint is making a movie and makes contact with the crowd, he has proved to love and relate to children and people in general.

Eastwood has had different horses in his movies. In his cinema filmed in the Boise, Idaho vicinity, his horse's name was Buster. Buster had three stunt doubles: Baldy, Cocoa, and Dandy. Clint employed a horse trainer, Alan Cartwright. Cartwright saved the horse, Baldy from slaughter. He bought the horse for $150.00 and nursed it back to health to appear in the movie. The stunts in Bronco Billy were fairly dangerous. The fire in the big-top and Clint's boarding a moving train from horseback were examples.

CHAPTER THIRTEEN
BUREAU OF LAND MANAGEMENT

Free roaming Mustangs are protected by the BLM and manages the wild Mustang populations. There is some controversy between free ranging Mustangs and the ranchers' livestock over lands and resources. The question is whether the free ranging Mustangs are a native species or an introduced invasive species. Adoption of range Mustangs has been popular. When the wild herds become overpopulated, the feral horses are rounded up and put up for adoption by the federal government. The ponies are held in temporary holding areas. The ideal situation is when the Mustangs are placed in permanent homes. The worst scenario is for them to be sold and slaughtered for horsemeat.

The Bureau of Land Management's job was to protect and manage the herds, but the Taylor Grazing Act had passed in 1934 to regulate the cattle industry, also. Horses and burros were not much value to the cattle man. Instead, they were outlaws and not much appreciated by the cattle ranchers.

In the 1950's, people became outraged over the treatment of wild horses and burros by mustangers. After capture, the animals are placed in the jurisdiction of the BLM.

In 1959, Congress passed the "Wild Horse Annie Act" to provide for the humane treatment of wild horses on federal lands protecting free-roaming Mustangs that later became State Law. Many wild horses around the Carson City and Reno areas remain under the jurisdiction of the Nevada State Estray laws that did little to prevent the inhumane treatment of feral horses.

The law was passed after finding abuse in capture methods like shooting the Mustangs from an airplane and poisoning them. The Wild Horse Annie Act prohibited hunting wild horses and burros from motor vehicles, but provided no program to manage wild horses. The first wild horse preserve was established in 1962

Jenny (Burro)
Eminent Domain

n Central Nevada on Nellis Air Force Base, named "the Nevada Wild Horse Range." The area had been previously closed to the public. In Utah, spirited Mustangs ran at a gallop for miles from the Swasey Mountains across the plains. Stallions led the mares and colts, driven by thundering helicopters overhead. The choppers herded the terrified ponies as they ran into a trap and the gate closed on them. They panicked. Horse families were divided and shipped to separate facilities; they lost their freedom and were isolated. Ponies were captured in 10 Western states over 32 million acres of public land. When the BLM had finished, they had surrounded and captured 50,000 wild horses, leaving 32,000 Mustangs still living on the range. Many think that the BLM Wild Horse & Burro Program is out of control and is headed for crises. Adoption rates have fallen and the cost of maintenance is high. Before 1971, airplanes made it useful to round-up wild feral horses, but many Mustangs met their demise because of them. Wild Mustangs were shot from airplanes as varmint outlaws. Round-ups capturing horses by the use of airplanes and helicopters terrorized the Mustangs.

The American Wild Horse Preservation Campaign is one of the groups that are fighting the round-up program. They say that it doesn't make sense, and doesn't work. They are upset that it costs the taxpayers money and the wild horses their freedom, sometimes their lives. They consider the round-up program to be insanity.

Investigation of the grazing areas proves that 82½ per cent of BLM land was allocated to livestock and only 17½ per cent allocated to the wild horses. NBC News reported that the wild horses were not treated equally. Some ranchers claim that the horses overgrazed and that the cattle are shorted food. Then in 1968, the Montana Pryor Mountains Wild Horse Range was established on BLM land by Interior Secretary Stewart Udall. In 1969, a Wild Horse Sanctuary was established.

Two Year Old Spanish Mustang
BLM Adoption Center in Nevada
Public Domain

In 1971, President Richard Nixon passed the Wild and Free-Roaming Horses and Burros Act of 1971. That year, 17,000 wild horses and 10,000 burros roamed the 10 Western states on BLM and Forest Service land, but not on National Parks and U.S. Fish and Wildlife Service land. Local livestock owners had to purchase permits for their horses and burros to graze on public lands. The law was apparent, but the budget had been overspent. The protection of wild horses and burros was not mapped out.

The Wild Free-Roaming Horse and Burros Act states that the wild horse and burros shall be protected from branding, capture, death, and harassment. Activists maintain that they are subject to just that. Injuries of horses have occurred during BLM round-ups and death; they only attribute 1% deaths in round-ups.

The fact remains that there are growing populations of wild horses and burros in the desert and that their population doubles every four years. The BLM maintains less than 32,000 feral horses. Livestock owners had to claim and permit their private horses and burros grazing on the public lands or lose ownership of them. After the law passed, any unbranded free-roaming horses and burros became the property of the federal government. Herd areas for wild horses and boundaries were set without doing research to study behavior patterns, migratory routes, water resources, annual food sources, and reproductive rates. Sometimes maps for the wild horses overlapped with those for cattle.

Wild-roaming horses are living symbols of Nevada's historic and pioneer spirit of the American West. The BLM is the agency responsible for managing wild horses on public lands and has authority to mandate the care of and to dispose of excess wild burros and horses according to the rules and regulations of the of the 1971 Wild Free-Roaming Horses and Burros Act, as the wild horses increase in numbers, in holding facilities and on the range.

Up for adoption from the BLM
Public Domain

The BLM, horse advocacy groups, and the public that are interested in wild horses struggle to find ways to deal with the problem. Unbranded and unclaimed free-roaming horses are protected and managed by the BLM in the western United States by the Wild Free-Roaming Horse and Burro Act of 1971. Any excess animals are offered to the general public by adoption.

Animals living anywhere else are not included in the 1971 Wild Free-Roaming Horse and Burro Protection Act. Any other horses were at this time and forever excluded. Protection remains only in the color coded herd areas of the map. The Virginia Range surrounding Carson City and Reno, Nevada are non-BLM and not protected, which are instead protected by the State of Nevada Stray laws. Most herds in major Nevada National Parks are protected and those herds living on County lands in the West. Protection of wild horse herds caused an increase in populations.

The BLM is the primary authority that oversees the management and protection of Mustang herds on public lands. The United States Forest Service administers additional wild burro and horse territory.

The National Wild Horse and Burro Center at Palomino Valley outside of Reno has 5,000 wild horses penned. Nevada is home to over 50 percent of the nation's wild horses and burros. Horses are adopted out under certain requirements. PVC is the largest BLM adoption facility in the country as the adoption center for wild horses and burros gathered from the public lands in Nevada and other near-by states.

The Little Book Cliffs area was established in 1974 in an area of Colorado as a wild horse preserve.

Herd areas of the map were poorly picked for vegetation and water resources. Taking all of the conditions into mind, migratory routes and behavior patterns were not studied and too hastily picked. It turned out to be a checkerboard area with private

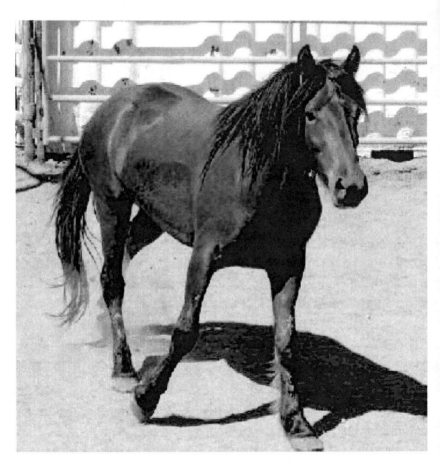

Two Year Old Mare at Adoption Center
Public Domain

land mixed in and was a mess. Horses living in the wrong areas did not receive protection.

In the adoption program, horses and burros are adopted out by private parties and are transitioned onto farms and ranches. A Mustang just off the range is 100% horse. Adopting such a horse educated the owner about horse behavior of the mind that a wild-born horse possesses. To help one transition to domestic life does the animal a kindness. Most adopters can recall the time that an untamed Mustang allowed them to touch it.

The BLM is a United States agency with a large mission to maintain the health and productivity of the public lands of America for use and enjoyment in the present and future generations. It administers over 245 million acres of land surface and handles more land than any other government agency. Most of the BLM land is located in the 12 Western states and Alaska. It manages 700 million acres of BLM land of underground mining regions across the nation. Its mission of public land resources in the Federal Land Policy and Management Act of 1976 delegated management resource use of energy, livestock grazing, recreation, timber harvesting, and protection of cultural and historical resources as the agency's duties in the 27 million acre conservation system.

In 1978, several holding areas and adoption centers were established. The Public Rangelands Improvement Act (PRIA) amended WHRHBA to stress the multiple use concepts of public lands and to authorize the removal of horses when necessary to provide a thriving economical balance to protect range animals and an inventory of the wild horse and burro herds.

The Eugene Wild Horse and Adoption Center opened in September of 1978. By 1986, it had adopted out over 3,000 horses and 150 burros. In 1991, a Wild Burro Ranch was created on BLM land, in Montana by Interior Secretary Udall. It was first managed by the agency and local advocates.

139

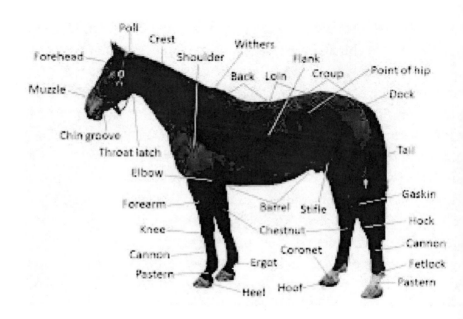

Horse Anatomy
Photo Courtesy of Wikipeda.org

The BLM conducted their own review of their round-ups from videos. Their findings were: Helicopters pursued horses too close for too long. There was extensive use of electric prods, kicking, and pinning horses in gates and twisting of tails during loading. The decision for better treatment of horses was split.

In 2013, a restraining order halting the round-up was issued after photos were produced of a helicopter driving horses through a barb-wire fence. Changes were ordered in the BLM procedures.

The wilderness area comprises 8.7 million acres, including 16 National Monuments that make up 4.8 million acres. The BLM has an annual budget of $1 billion dollars and 10,000 full time employees. It generates more revenue than it spends. Billions of dollars in revenue comes from off shore gas and oil development.

The agency is aimed at the conservation of the managed lands and resources and reconnecting Americans to the outdoors. BLM facilitates renewable development of geothermal, solar, and wind energy. It encourages youth and families to explore, learn, and visit the public lands. The agency tries to control the effect of climate change on Americans' quality of life.

BLM dispatches fire fighters in the West over millions of acres to protect their lands, including humans and wild horses and other wildlife. They are equipped with heavy fire engines, experienced crews, helicopter crews, dozers, water tenders, fire dispatchers and also prevention staff.

During hot dry summers, fire agencies are overworked fighting fires on America's public lands, which are started by campers, cigarettes, and lightning strikes. Fires kill fauna, flora, and burn thousands of acres. The BLM staffs a crew to conduct hazardous fuels reduction, go to wild-land fire incident response and pre and post burn monitoring.

Horses of Today
Photo Courtesy of Wikipedia.org

CHAPTER FOURTEEN
MODERN HORSES

Since the beginning of time man has established a symbiotic relationship with the horse. Spaniards introduced the Horse to the Americas. The Native Americans distributed them across America. The white man came into the picture and possessed the horse and making it widespread. A friend to humans, horses are one of the few animals on earth that can be ridden.

Cow horses are still used on the western range. Horses are bred and raised on ranches with select breeding. A specific breed is targeted. Cayuse Ranch is one example. The West was begun with homesteads, farms and ranches. From the late 1800's into modern times the cowboys' means of transportation was the horse. Horses are content to graze in green pastures and are at home being domesticated as much as in the wild.

Ranchers in the mid-west in the 1900's pursued breeding of the Spanish blood lines. Bob Brislawn owned the Cayuse Ranch near Oshoto, Wyoming, managed by his son, Emmett. Another breeder was Ilo Belsky from Tuthill, South Dakota who raised Spanish Mustangs that had originally been driven up North on Texas drives back in 1885. Ilo had bred a strain of Spanish Mustangs to near perfection. His herd had the remnant of Spanish Jennets. Belsky called them Spanish Barbs.

Their colors were dun, blue-roan, and grulla. Belsky, the Brislawn brothers, and Jones managed to restore the gene pool and save the Spanish Mustang horse type in America. These men scoured the BLM, every Indian reservation and Mustang ranch in search of the best Spanish Mustang type. In 1957, Brislawn announced the formation of the first Colonial Spanish Horse Association that listed 3,000 registered horses, the first colonist Spanish horse association.

A breed of horses could be defined as a group of horses that have a common origin, which possess certain distinctive and uniformly transmitted characteristics that are not common to other horses. Brislawn described Appaloosas, Buckskins, Palominos, Paints, and Pintos as color phases of the Barb or Spanish Barb.

Today, Emmett's Cayuse Ranch still breeds excellent Spanish Mustang Horses. The Spanish Mustang registry was first established using excellent sires and dams. They maintained a select herd of Spanish Mustangs.

The horses were numbered beginning with a SMR-1, in sequence. It began with Buckshot SMR-1, Ute SMR-2, and Bally SMR-3, etcetera. San Domingo, a red roan Medicine Hat stallion obtained from the Navajo Indians, who had captured the horse in the wild earlier. The stallion, San Domingo filled the position of SMR-4. Straight Arrow, the mottled roan son of Ute took the spot of SMR-5. With 3,000 registered Spanish Mustangs on the Cayuse Ranch, Belsky, Brislawn and Jones had laid the ground-work for horse registries. A gene pool exists for breeding Spanish Mustangs.

Mustangs no longer face extinction. Breeder's dedication has created interest in the Spanish Mustang. Although the wild Mustang may never roam free in the American desert again, the illusive Spanish Mustangs have earned their place in our society

Horses were readily useful during WWI in 1914-1917. Besides use for America, Militaries from England, France and Italy came to America to purchase horses for their cavalry units. Europeans bought thousands of America's western mounts. The shortage pushed the price to over $150.00 per horse. Sources said that over $1,000,000 was spent on American horses shipped overseas to the European front, which depleting the number of free-roaming horses in the American desert, but it would not be long before the US Army would become mechanized.

Modern Arabian
Photo Courtesy of Wikipedia.org

American Indian, Joe Medicine Crow sat in the sweat lodge and listened to the warrior tales told by his elders and entered the service as an Army scout for the 103rd Infantry Division during World War II. In combat, he wore his war paint under his uniform and his sacred feather beneath his helmet in the tradition of a Crow warrior. He touched an enemy German enemy, disarmed him, and counted first and second coups.

Joe led a night raid, stole German horses and sang a Crow Indian war song of honor, as he rode away. Joseph Medicine Crow was the recipient of the Bronze Star Medal, the Legion of Honor, and the Presidential Medal of Freedom. He is a member of the Crow Nation, patriot, brave warrior and the last Chief of the Crow Nation a historian and author of Native American history. The Crow Indians are a proud race and served in the Army as strong warriors. They served until 1947.

The American Albino Horses, American White Horses and Ponies originated in Naper, Nebraska in the United States. They have light blue to dark blue, almost black eyes. The breed stands from 8 to 17 hands high. The American Albinos are utilized as riding and utility horses. Their fair white skin color makes them attractive as horses on exhibit, flag bearers, and for parades.

Appaloosas originated in the Pacific Northwest and were bred from the Jennet horse. They have white blotches on the hips, loins, and midriff with egg-shaped dark spots over the blotches. The eyes show more white than most other breeds. The skin is mottled. Hoofs are vertically striped black and white. Appaloosas are parade, pleasure, race and stock horses.

Arabian Horses originated in the Arabian Peninsula. Their coat colors are bay, black, chestnut and white. White marks on the head or legs are common. The skin color is always dark. Arabians are docile horses used for pleasure, racing, saddle, show and stock.

Friendly Persuasion
Author Photo

American Buckskin Horses were developed in the United States. Their coat colors are buckskin, grulla, and red dun and they have a dorsal stripe and a transverse stripe over the withers and zebra-like stripes on the legs, indicating that they descend from the Spanish Mustang. Buckskins are used as pleasure horses, and stock horses. Buckskins with white above the hocks are disqualified.

The American Paint Horse originated in the United States. Coat colors are white plus any other color. Paints are a loyal, hard working mount. The Paint had pronounced markings of white or dark markings. The overo is a Paint. The overo or dark Paint Horse had light markings and the toviano had characteristics of both overo and toviano. The prominence of an overo may be dark on white. On the back of an overo horse the white color will not cross between the withers and the tail. In the overo the white areas arise from the belly and underneath. Coat patterns do not always work neatly into the overo and toviano categories, some have both patterns. With toviano the white areas on the back extend downward. In judging, no discrimination is made for eye color, but they are disqualified for white stockings above the hock. The American Paint Horses are used for pleasure, racing and show.

The American Pinto Horses' ancestors originated in Spain and were brought to America. Coats are half colors and half white with spots well placed. Pinto in Spanish means paint or a blemish. Most Paints are Pintos, but Pintos are not always Paints. The American Pinto Association has different breeding rules than the American Paint Association. Pinto is a spotted horse and a breed of horse bred for the musculature similar to a Quarter Horse, and for unique coloring. Pintos were bred from Arabian stock and resemble the Paint. Mustangs' colors indicated various breeds.

The American Saddle Horses originated in Fayette County, Kentucky. Coat colors are bay, black, brown, chestnut and gray. Saddle Horses produce an easy ride.

Bay Roan Stud
Author photo

The Galiceno Horses originated in Northwestern Spain and were brought to America by the Conquistadors, but were not introduced in America as a breed until 1958. Common colors are bay, black, brown, chestnut, dun, gray or palomino. Galiceno Horses stand 12 to 13 hands high and. The Galicenos weigh 625 to 700 pounds and are fine riding horses. Galicenos are disqualified for registration if they have albino, paint or pinto coloration.

The American Gotland Horse originated in Sweden in the Baltic Islands of Gotland. Their coat colors are bay, black, brown, chestnut, dun, palomino, and roan, with some blanket and leopard markings. American Gotlands average 51" high and range from 11 to 14 hands. Gotlands are used for harness racing, jumping, and riding. Pintos and gaudy marking disqualify them.

The Missouri Fox Trotting Horses originated in the United States. These horses are normally sorrel or any other color. The Missouri Fox Trotters are distinguished by the fox trot gait. They are used for trail riding, pleasure, and stock horses. These horses are disqualified if they cannot fox trot.

Morgan Horses originated in the United States in New England. Coat colors are bay, black, brown, and chestnut. White markings are acceptable on the face, but white stocking above the hocks are not, in judging. They are used as saddle and stock horses and have qualities of easy to raise, docility and endurance.

Palomino Horses originated in the United States. The Palomino horses descended from Arabian and Barb horses and are a gorgeous golden color with a silver mane and tail and white face. Palominos are an all around horse good for riding, ranching and rodeos, known for their speed and endurance.

Paso Fino Horses originated in the Caribbean and have since been registered with the American Paso Fino Pleasure Horse Association. Their coats are almost any color, bay, chestnut, or black, the most common and sometimes Palominos or Pin**tos**

Golden Palomino Mare & Foal
Photo Courtesy of Kvetina-Marie - flickr.com

appear. Paso Finos are ridden for cutting, pleasure, and parades. In the Spanish, Paso Fino means fine step. In the Paso Fino gait, the legs of the same side move together, but the hind hoof strikes the ground a second before the front hoof, producing a four-beat gait.

The Peruvian Paso Horse originated in Peru, but was imported into the United States. Their coats may be any color, yet solid colors are preferred. They walk Paso trot, broken paced, and canter naturally five gaited. These horses are used for endurance, parades, and riding pleasure. Horses with coarseness, extreme height, or light forequarters are disqualified from competition.

The Pony of the Americas originated in the United States in Mason City, Iowa. Their coat coloration is like Appaloosas. The ponies have the characteristics of Arabians and Quarter Horses, but are a similar size, their height ranging from 46 to 54 inches. They are used as western–style riding ponies for children. The ponies are disqualified for registration if they do not qualify within the height range or do not have Appaloosa coloration, which includes mottled skin and whites in the eyes or have Pinto markings.

Quarter Horses originated in the United States. Common coat colors are bay, black, brown, chestnut, palomino, roan and sorrel. Quarter Horses have small, alert ears and usually heavily muscled cheek and jaw. They are well muscled and powerfully built. Quarter horses are used as pleasure, race, and stock horses.

The Shetland Ponies came from the Shetland Islands. Their coats may be any color, broken or solid. They are miniature horses. In the breed register, two classes are recognized: 43 inches and under and 43-46" in height. Children ride Shetlands. They are also used in pony harness, as racing ponies and for roadsters.

The Spanish Barb Horses originated in the United States in Oshoto, Wyoming. Their coats may be any color, solid or broken, except toviano. The Barb may have five vertebra, although most modern horses have developed six large vertebrae, with the

White Donkey
Author Photo

exception of Arabians and descendants of the Spanish Mustangs which have five vertebra. They have short ears, round leg bones, and a low set tail and are used for cow ponies and trail riding.

The Spanish Jennet horse was developed in Spain, bred from the Iberian horse and used by the Spanish light Cavalry. The Spanish Mustang is a probable descendent of the Spanish Jennet horse. This fine animal is a well proportioned horse of moderate build and height.

The Jennet has a deep chest and broad muscular loins and has a powerful spirit. Its characteristics are an even temperament and a smooth gait; the Paso gait of the Spanish Jennet is inherited. The four beat lateral gaits with each foot contacting the ground independently produce a tapping sound in regular sequence and an unbroken rhythm. The Jennet gives a smooth ride at a running walk, performs well at a canter and gallop and is an agile and athletic pony capable of many disciplines.

The Standard-bred Horses originated in the United States. The common coat colors are bay, black, brown, chestnut, dun, and gray. These horses are less leggy, more rugged, and smaller than thoroughbreds. Standardbreds are used as harness horses in horse shows, for harness racing, pacing or trotting

Tennessee Walking Horses originated in the United States. Coat colors are bay, black, brown, chestnut, gray or golden, with white markings on face and legs. Characteristics are their running walk. Their use is a plantation, walking, pleasure, and show horses.

Thoroughbred Horses originated in England, but were imported to the United States. Common coat colors are bay, black, brown, and chestnut, and sometimes gray or roan. White markings are common on the face and legs. These horses are noted for their long, straight, and well muscled legs. Thoroughbreds are used in hunting, and as polo, race, saddle, and stock horses.

154

Morgan Horse
Photo Courtesy of Wikipedia.org

The Welsh Pony originated in Wales and was imported to America. Their coat may be any color. White markings are not popular. Welsh Ponies are intermediate size between the light horse and Shetland pony size. Height stipulates two divisions: Division A. cannot exceed 12.2 hands and division B. cannot be over 14 hands. These ponies are used for hunting, mounts for children, pacing, and trail riding.

There are 350 breeds of horses today in four major groups of horses: light horses, work horses, ponies, and feral horses. Feral horses are wild like a Mustang. Light horses and ponies have gained popularity in America. Horses are classified according to draft horses, light horses and ponies pertaining to build, size, and use. Light horses stand from 14.2 to 17 hands high (a hand is 4"). Light horses have small bones and weigh 900-1400 pounds. Examples of light horses are Arabians, Morgans, Quarter Horses, Saddlebreds, Tennessee Walkers, and Thoroughbreds. Ponies are under 14.2 hands and weigh up to 900 pounds. Ponies range from 12 ½ to 14 ½ hands, averaging 14 hand spans and weigh from 725-800 pounds. They are a sturdy horse and can be ridden, driven or used as a good pack horse. Draft horses stand from 14.2 to 17.2 hands high. They are used for heavy work and hauling.

The pace or gait is a natural or acquired means of movement of the horses feet and legs. The amble is a slow lateral gait different from the pace by a slower more broken cadence. The amble gait is not shown like the stepping pace, but a lateral four beat gait, done in showy animated fashion, with set chin, folding of the knees and flexing the hocks for showiness. There is a break as the feet impact, making it a four beat gait done at slow speed.

The canter is a slowed three beat gait. The diagonal legs are paired and produce a single beat between the successive beats of the opposing legs. The lope is a slow canter and a slow gait in which the head is held low.

Paint Horse
Photo Courtesy of Wikipedia.org

The gallop or run is a fast four beat gait in which the feet strike the ground severely. Then, like the trot, there is a moment where all four feet are aloft. The gallop is a fast natural gait of both thoroughbreds and wild horses.

The pace is a two beat fast gait where both feet on the same side start and stop at the same time. The feet rise slightly above the ground. At one point, all of the feet float in the air.

The rack is a fast, flashy, four-beat gait also called the "single-foot." It is rarely executed voluntarily, but more on command. The gait is characterized by a display of knee action and speed. The gait is pleasant for the rider, but wears the horse down.

The running walk is a slow, four-beat gait with the break in rhythm that occurs between diagonal fore and hind feet. The running walk is a gait that can be maintained endlessly. It is done with great ease giving comfort to both horse and rider. The walk is a flat-footed four-beat, natural, slow gait.

The trot is a diagonal, natural, rapid gait when a front foot and the opposing hind foot strike the ground at the same time. For a brief moment all of the feet are off the ground and the horse is airborne.

There are many horse breeders and many breeds of horses, today in America: the American Miniature, American Paint, American Saddle, Appaloosa, Arabian, Belgian, Haflinger, Hanoverian, Moral, Morgan, Mustang, Palomino, Paso-Fino, Pinto, Pony of the Americas, Quarter Horse, Standard-bred, Tennessee Walking, Thoroughbred, Welsh Cob and Welsh Pony.

Heavy Horses are Draft Horses and large horses weigh as much as 2,000 pounds. These are strong with large bones and sturdy legs. Some examples are Belgian, Clydesdale, Shire, Percherons, and Suffolk horses. Shetland ponies are not much larger than 58 inches tall and smaller than any horse. Examples are Caspian, Fjord, Halflinger, and Shetland.

Beach Ponies
Photo Courtesy of Wikipedia.org

Humans and horses have had a symbiotic relationship since ancient times. Asians most probably domesticated horses 4,000 years ago. Horses and man have been linked for millennia. They are usually named and are quite intelligent, friendly and good companions deemed the 14th smartest animal. Horses are capable of learning tricks. A good example was Roy Roger's Trigger. Horses can learn to count. Remarkably, they have a good memory.

Horses should be fed regularly morning, noon, and night and to be fed legume hay roughage. Horses require roughage for digestion. Long hay and grain is a good mixture. Feed may be home-mixed or commercial. Grain is also an excellent feed. A grain ration is better fed first followed by roughage. Rolled oats and alfalfa pellets are a good feed. They should be fed vitamins and minerals, also.

Horses are kept in sheds or horse barns. Horses anticipate a regular feeding time and feed better in the cool of the morning and at night and should be fed an adequate amount of feed and be well cared for. Sixty million tons of commercial feeds are marketed every year. Feed prices are regulated through competition.

Horses require ample quantities of clean, cool, fresh water. They normally drink 10 to 12 gallons of water a day. Various conditions affect the amount that they drink. Water, like feed, should be administered at the same time daily. Watering times vary among horsemen. Horses are to be given water before, after, and during feeding. Ample water is needed. During hot weather, water should be given between feedings. If a horse is worked hard, a small amount of water should be given, but they should not be watered heavily if it is hot. It may cause the horse to founder. Horses should not be allowed to drink too much before going out to work.

Small Wild Horse Herd
Photo Courtesy of Wikipedia.org

Horses should have clean bedding and proper ventilation and be bathed and curried often. The horse owners groom their animals regularly; they take pride in their horses and give them constant care. They love their animals and dote on them.

Although there is but one species of horse, there are 400 various breeds. Some horses are domesticated, others run wild. Feral horses are descendants of animals that were once tame and now run wild in herds. Three or more wild horses make up a herd.

A single stallion leads a herd composed of mares (females) and their foals (young). Mares closely guard their offspring. Mares with foals are plentiful in the country. Colts frolic and like to kick up their heels. Colts run in order to race each other and frolic. As the young foals reach about two years of age, the stallion runs them off. The colts join other young males until the time that they can take command of their own band of fillies.

Horses are used for work and are also ridden for pleasure. There are more people riding horses now in America than ever before. Horses are ridden for pleasure. Horse handlers have entered into the production end involving judging, breeding, feeding, miscellaneous management, marketing, and selling. Raising horses can be a full time operation. Saddle clubs are increasing in America. Horses are judged by class, like Purebreds and Quarter horses, saddle horses and work horses. Quality stallions are mated with purebred mares for the highest quality foals. Breeding may be repeated in order to get the sort of progeny desired. A good pedigree gives the purebred the right kind of identity. In judging a good horse, every aspect of the animal is considered.

Pastures for horses should be spacious with not too large of a concentration of horses. The pasture should have good fences of woven wire with mesh so small that the horses cannot get their feet through it. Good pasture land with the proper fences keep horses off of the roads and promote better relations with their neighbors.

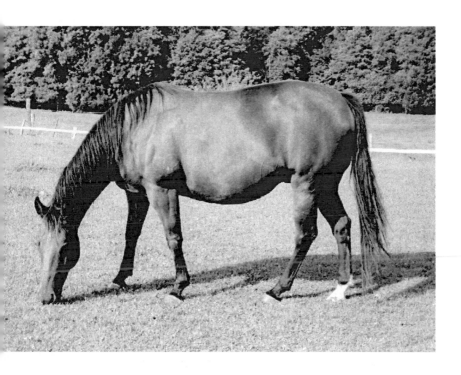

Quarter Horse
Photo Courtesy of Wikipedia.org

Metal fences and padlocks should be strong conventional steel or aluminum.

Horses should be protected against diseases and parasites. A good veterinarian should be retained for regular check-ups. Strict sanitation should be adhered to. Disease and parasite control is a must for healthy horses. Horses must be kept healthy and happy. In warm weather, the animals should have ample exercise, shade and water.

In order to breed horses, they have to be healthy. A healthy stallion should breed a healthy mare. A pregnant mare should have good sanitation. A mare in good weather should be allowed to foal in a secluded pasture away from other live-stock. The foal should be kept clean and sanitary. During bad weather, the mare should be kept in a roomy well lighted, well ventilated box stall with clean bedding. The foal should be checked out by a veterinarian. All soiled bedding should be removed and the stall sanitized with lye.

Horses mostly have a good temperament. They are gentle and easy to ride with good dispositions and are beautiful animals and quite majestic.

Horses vary in size from the Shetland pony to the huge Quarter Horse. Since ancient times man has possessed horses. Horses are highly practical and have always been utilitarian.

Horses and man have formed a special bond in a symbiotic relationship and are excellent pets and affectionate animals. They jump and race for sport, but mainly are used for riding pleasure. Horses make wonderful pets and companions. Those that are abused are handled by the Society for the Prevention of Cruelty to Animals. Horses are a friend to mankind.

Bay Horse
Photo Courtesy of Wikipedia.org

Sorraia Horse
Photo Courtesy of Wikipedia.org

Bibliography

Bains, Rae, *Indians of the Plains*, Mahwah, New Jersey, Troll Associates, 1985.

Capps, Benjamin, *The Great Chiefs*, Time-Life, Alexandria, Virginia, 1975.

Convis, Charles L., *Warriors & Chiefs of the Old West*, Pioneer Press, Inc., Carson City, 1996.

Ensminger, M.E., *Horses and Horsemanship*, Interstate Printers and Publishers, Inc., Danville, Illinois, 1989.

Fehrenbach, T.R., *Comanches, The History of a People*, Anchor Books, New York, 1974.

Grant, Bruce, *Concise Encyclopedia of American Indians*, Random House, New York, 1989.

Gwynne, S.C., *Empire of the Summer Moon*, Scribner, New York, 2010.

Hagan, William T., *Quanah Parker, Comanche Chief*, University of Oklahoma Press, Norman, 1993.

Haines, Francis, *The Buffalo*, Thomas Y. Crowell Company, New York, 1970.

Haines, Francis, *Appaloosa, the Spotted Horse in Art and History*, Caballus Publishers, Lansing, 1963.

Kays, D.J., *The Horse*, A.S. Barnes & Co., New York, 1953.

Inter-Tribal Council of Nevada, *Newe: A Western Shoshone History*, University of Utah Printing Service, Salt Lake, 1976.

Lee, Nelson, *Three Years Among the Comanches*, The Narrative Press, Santa Barbera, 2001.

Liljeblad, Sven, *The Idaho Indians in Transition, 1805-1960*, Idaho State University, Pocatello, Idaho, 1972.

Lund, Bill, *The Comanche Indians*, Bridgestone Books, Mankato, Minnesota, 1997.

Mails, Thomas E., *The Mystic Warriors of the Plains*, Mallard Press, New York,, 1991.

Madsen, Brigham D., *The Northern Shoshoni*, Caxton Printers, Ltd., Caldwell, Idaho, 1980.

Mooney, Martin J., *The Comanche Indians*, Chelsea House Publishers, New York, 1993.

Neeley, Bill, *The Last Comanche Chief, The Life and Times of Quanah Parker*,

O'Neal, Bill, *Best of the West*, Lincolnwood, Illinois, Publications International, Ltd., 2006.

Utley, Robert M., *Encyclopedia of the American West*, Wings Books, New York, 1997.

Utley, Robert M., *Lone Star Justice*, Berkley Book Publishing Company, New York, 2002.

Wallace, Ernest & Hoebel, E. Adamson, The *Comanches, Lords of the Southern Plains*, University of Oklahoma Press, Norman, 1986.

Whistler, Clark, *Indians of the United States*, Doubleday, Garden City, New York, 1966.

Wyman, Walker D., *The Wild Horse of the West*, Caxton Printers, Ltd., Caldwell, Idaho, 1945.

Citing Electronic
Publications

<http://www.angelfire.com/realm/shades/nativeamericans/bison.htm>
<http://www.ansi.okstate.edu/breeds/horses/cayuseindian/>
<http://www.blm.gov/wo/st/en/info/About_BLM.html>
<http://www.biography.com/people/gene-autry-9542056>
<http://www.britannica.com/EBchecked/topic/272329/horse-racing>
<http://www.csp.org/communities/docs/fikes-nac_history.html>
<http:///www.digital.library.okstate.edu/encyclopedia/entries/c/ch045.html>
<http://www.digital.library.okstate.edu/encyclopedia/entries/f/fo038.html>
<http://www.en.wikipedia.org/wiki/Rodeo>
<http://www.en.wikipedia.org/wiki/Spanish_Jennet_Horse>
<http://www.footnote.com/page/1928_quanah_parker_the_comanche_nation/>
<http://www.indiancountrynews.com/wildlife-resources-sections-menu-
118/1339-the-wild-horses-of-ute-country>
<http://www.infoplease.comce6/society/A0834977.html>
<http://www.legendsofamerica.com/na-commanche.html>
<http://www.loc.gov/rr/program/bib/ourdocs/Indian.html>
<http://www.muskingum.edu/~rmunkres/indians/Indians.html>
<http://www.naiaonline.org/naia-library/articles/professional-rodeo-horses-are-
bred-to-buck/#sthash.mHXxDLsq.dpbs>
<http://www.netnebraska.org/basic-page/television/wild-horses-native-
americans>
<http://www.shire-horse.org.uk>
<http://www.snowowl.com/peoplecomanche.html>
<http://www.spanishvisionfarm.com/Articles/History/conquistadors.html>
<http://www.texasranger.org/history/RangersRepublic.htm>
 <http://www.tshaonline.org/handbook/online/artitles/ayc02>
<http://www.tshaonline.org/handbook/online/articles/btao1>

INDEX

Born in Lexington, Nebraska, Author Robert Bolen, B.A. has a degree in Archeology/Anthropology. In an Archeology class, he was informed that because of his Mongolian eye-fold, he was part Indian. In 1755, a Bolen ancestor was taken captive by Delaware Indians and later rescued with her baby daughter, Robb's Great, Great, Grandmother. When rescued, the poor girl (just 17) was scalped, but she lived. A French scalp was the size of a silver dollar. Family says she combed her hair to hide the scar and lived to be well over one hundred years of age. Bolen's served under George Washington in the American Revolution. In 1777, the author's ancestors erected Fort Bolin, near Cross Creek, Pennsylvania for protection from Indian attacks. Two ancestors were killed in Kentucky by Shawnee Indians allied to the British. Great Granddad Gilbert Bolen rode with the Ohio Fourth Cavalry in the Civil War under General Sherman. In 1866, Gilbert brought his wife and six children west to Nebraska in a Conestoga wagon. Gran-dad Denver Colorado Bolen knew Buffalo Bill Cody in western Nebraska. Bolen is an authority on Indian artifacts and glass trade beads. Robb and Dori Bolen reside in Nampa, Idaho, near Boise. Robb owns the website, Fort Boise Bead Trader.com.

More Books
by Robert D. Bolen

Smoke Signals & Wagon Tracks

American Indian Tribes of Idaho

**Blackfeet Raiders
Nomads of the North**

The Horse Indians

The Lakota Sioux Indians

The Medicine Crow Indians

**"The Snake People"
The Northern Shoshoni Indians**

**War Chief Paulina
& His Renegade
Band of Paiutes**

The Paiute Indian Nation

Chief Joseph and the Indian Wars

Photos of Books Written
by Robert D. Bolen

Robert D. Bolen

CHIEF JOSEPH AND THE INDIAN WARS

THE LATEST BOOK WRITTEN BY ROBERT D. BOLEN

PHOTOGRAPHS COURTESY OF

AZUSA Publishing, LLC

3575 S. Fox Street

Englewood, CO 80110

Email: azusa@azusapublishing.com

Phone Toll-free: 888-783-0077

Phone/Fax: 303-783-0073

Graphic Design Services

Provided by

DESIGNER

Cover Design

Book Layout

Text and Page Formatting

Editing

Photo Clarification and Enhancement

Etc.

Bonnie Fitzpatrick

208.249.2635

bjfitz 777@msn.com

CPSIA information can be obtained
at www.ICGtesting.com
Printed in the USA
FSOW02n0420220216
17143FS